Fit for Mission?
Church

Expanded edition

Being Catholic Today

Patrick O'Donoghue
Bishop of Lancaster

THE CATHOLIC TRUTH SOCIETY
PUBLISHERS TO THE HOLY SEE

Cardinale Renato Raffaele Martino

Presidente del Pontificio Consiglio della Giustizia e della Pace

23 September 2008

Your Excellency,

I am pleased to acknowledge the receipt of your letter dated 2 September 2008, wherein you kindly enclosed a copy of your recent publication entitled *Fit for Mission? Church: Being Catholic Today*. Thank you very much for your consideration in this regard.

The text is very well put together, incorporating all of the main elements of Catholic social thought. I am confident that it will be a useful and helpful resource to the local Church of Lancaster and beyond. Congratulations and many blessings upon your ministry as shepherd and teacher.

With renewed sentiments of my esteem and gratitude, I am

Sincerely yours in the Lord,

Renato Raffaele Cardinal Martino

H.E. Most Reverend Patrick O'Donoghue
Bishop of Lancaster
Bishop's Apartment
Cathedral House
Balmoral Road
Lancaster LA1 3BT
UNITED KINGDOM

00120 Città del Vaticano - Tel. 0039 06 6987.9908 - Fax 0039 06 6988 7205 - E-mail rmartino @ justpeace.va

3

CONGREGATIO
PRO CLERICIS

Vatican City, 18th September 2008

Prot. N. 20082694

His Lordship, the Rt. Rev. Patrick O'Dononghue
Bishop of Lancaster
Cathedral House
Balmoral Road
Lancaster LA1 3BT
GREAT BRITAIN.

Your Lordship,

This Congregation has gratefully received the copies you forwarded of the documents *Fit for Mission? Schools* and *Fit for Mission? Church.*

The Dicastery has already expressed it's appreciation of *Fit for Mission? Schools* in our previous correspondence of 15th December 2007, (Prot. N. 20073260). It is still somewhat amazed at the reaction the text provoked as it was both an appropriate and legitimate exercise of Episcopal authority by a Successor of the Apostles charged by God, and by the Church, to ensure that the Faith is transmitted correctly and in its entirety, to the People of God entrusted to his care. You were simply doing your duty in this regard.

It should go without saying that Catholic schools, as one of the primary vehicles for the this ongoing task, must be imbued with a Catholic ethos that is real and not simply imaginary. Your Lordship has realistically faced a situation that has been an oft repeated theme over many years, by the Faithful of your country in their correspondence with this Congregation. The Dicastery again lauds you for your courageous action.

The latest document in the series, *Fit for Mission? Church,* is hewn from the same rich vein as *Fit for Mission? Schools,* namely the Traditions of the Church as expressed in the Second Vatican Council and in the *Catechism of the Catholic Church*. In this latest text Your Lordship has provided an effective, practical instrument for advancing the much heralded *New Evangelization*. If this renewal of the Faith is to take root, it cannot remain a mere "slogan" but must be woven into the web of contemporary culture. *Fit for Mission? Church* gives much needed indication as to the means of accomplishing this great mission of the Church.

May the Lord continue to bless your efforts.

I take this opportunity to renew my sentiments of esteem and with every best wish, I remain,

Sincerely Yours in Christ,

✠Mauro Piacenza
Titular Archbishop of Vittoriana
Secretary

3

Congregazione per il Clero - 00120 Città del Vaticano - Tel. 06/69884151 - Fax: 06/69884845

4

Acknowledgements

I could not have attempted to write a work of this scope and depth without the inspiration and work of many others, pastors and theologians alike. I would particularly like to acknowledge the work of Pope John Paul II, Pope Benedict XVI, Avery Cardinal Dulles and Fr Aidan Nichols OP.

I recommend the following books and articles that have informed and inspired me in writing this document for your own further study and reflection:

Joseph Cardinal Ratzinger, *Principles of Catholic Theology*, Ignatius Press, 1987.

Avery Cardinal Dulles, 'Vatican II: The Myth & the Reality' in *America*. 24th February, 2003.

Avery Cardinal Dulles, 'From Ratzinger to Benedict' in *First Things*. February 2006.

Aidan Nichols OP, *The Thought of Benedict XVI*, Burns & Oates, 2005.

Aidan Nichols OP, *Beyond the Blue Glass*, Vol. 1. St Austin Press, 2002.

Contents

Preface

Sitting here at my desk in the Bishop's Apartment working on the expanded CTS edition of this latest document in the *Fit for Mission?* series, I ask myself the question that has been to the forefront of my mind since I put pen to paper: for whom have I written this document?

First and foremost I have written it for all of you who are serious about your faith, and who want to engage with the crucial questions of our generation through being faithful to the love and truth of God revealed in Jesus Christ, and safe-guarded by the Church.

I have also written it for all Catholics who love the Church and care deeply about the future of Catholicism in our country. I know that many of you share my sense of pressing responsibility to foster and promote an authentic Catholic identity, resisting the pressures to compromise, even abandon, the truths of our faith.

The hundreds of letters and emails I have received in response to my two *Fit for Mission?* documents have greatly encouraged me, knowing that there are priests, deacons, religious, lay men and women throughout our country who share my longing and urgent striving for the renaissance of the Catholic faith.

Finally, I have written it for all those who are seeking to know what is true about the Roman Catholic Church in the 21st century. In this document it is my hope that you will see a Church that seeks to make real in the world love of God and His love for humanity in his Son Jesus Christ.

Reflecting on the great issues facing us, I have become more and more convinced that many Catholics have forgotten that Pope John XXIII's intention in convening the Second Vatican Council was to renew the life of the Church through sensitively balancing change with the life-giving continuity of doctrinal, moral and liturgical truths.

During this time of confusion and wide-spread dissent at many levels of the Church, certainty is to be found through a prayerful, faithful and creative engagement with the Deposit of Faith presented in the documents of the Second Vatican Council and its great summary, the *Catechism of the Catholic Church*. This is the faith which Christ left to the Apostles and which they handed on to their successors.

The vision of *Fit for Mission? Church* is the vision of the Second Vatican Council. However, the questions and challenges that the Council Fathers saw in embryo, we now face in full force, such as the challenge of secular humanism, the question of moral values in a scientific-technological culture, and the increasing tensions caused by reason sundered from faith.

The Second Vatican Council began the great project of the Third Millennium - balancing continuity of identity with the need to change, so as to enable us to better proclaim the Gospel.

As you will see as you read through *Fit for Mission? Church*, there are sets of questions and action points after each section. An eleven session study course is also included to help you look at some key themes of my document. These have been included to help parish groups - and individuals - discuss and reflect on the many issues raised. The appendices include a list of definitions of ecclesial terms.

I would like to thank my team, consisting of clergy and laity, for their invaluable assistance and hard work in helping me produce this document - it could not have been done without them.

Finally, Pope Benedict XVI has declared 2008-2009 a year in which the Church celebrates the 2000th anniversary of the birth of St Paul. I would like to dedicate *Fit for Mission? Church* to this great missionary apostle whose life teaches us the importance of standing firm and holding fast to the Tradition taught by the Apostles:

> We must always give thanks to God for you, brothers and sisters beloved by the Lord, because God chose you as the first fruits for salvation through sanctification by the Spirit and through belief in the truth. (2 *Th* 2:13).

✣ **Patrick O'Donoghue, Bishop of Lancaster**

1   Introduction: Is our Church Alive with the Hope of Christ?

> Have no fear, nor be troubled, but in your hearts reverence Christ as Lord. Always be prepared to make a defence to anyone who calls you to account for the hope that is in you. (1 *P* 3:14-15).

In the light of my experience as a bishop, I should like to examine with you the reality of the Church in the 21st century.

Every year I have committed the majority of my diary to deanery and parish visitations. I consider my visitations to have been time very well spent. *Fit for Mission? Church* is the fruit of my experience of praying with my people, worshipping with them, sharing meals with them, teaching and learning with them over these past seven years.

I have been truly inspired by the commitment shown by so many of people, the long hours some clergy and people put into serving parishes, the faithful creativity brought to catechesis and liturgy, and the self-sacrifice willingly accepted in care for each other and the poor and needy.

Having said this, I am aware through the recent *Fit for Mission? Parish* review that there are very painful questions to ask because they are close to my heart, and I know they are also close to the hearts of many of you:

- Why have so many Catholics stopped coming to Mass? Where have all the young families and young people gone? Why do most families not pray together anymore?

- Why have so many Catholics rejected the mercy offered through the Sacrament of Reconciliation?

- Why are our seminaries almost empty, and our convents and monasteries closing?

- Why are there so few Catholic marriages?

- Why are many parents not sending their children to Catholic schools? Why have they lost confidence in our Catholic schools?

- Why did we stop speaking the truth with one voice? Why is there disharmony among us about the Catholic faith?

- Why are we so afraid to evangelise our society? Why have we lost passion and confidence in teaching the faith?

- Why does our Church feel so tired and worn out? What has dimmed the fire of hope within us?

1.1   God's Gift of Hope

Many who know me will tell you I am a man of hope. What do I mean by this? A man or woman of hope is not an optimist as such, in the sense of someone who, by temperament, chooses to seek out the positive in any situation. Hope is the expectation that our needs and dreams will reach fulfilment in God. As Pope Benedict XVI puts it in his encyclical on hope,

> ...we have been given hope, trustworthy hope, by virtue of which we can face our present: the present, even if it is arduous, can be lived and accepted if it leads towards a goal, if we can be sure of this goal, and if this goal is great enough to justify the effort of the journey. (Pope Benedict XVI, *Spe Salvi*, 1).

I am more convinced than ever that unless we are people of hope we will be unable to live joyfully the full reality of the Church. This hope is not an illusion, because it rests on the historical foundation of the paschal mystery - 'Christ has died, Christ is risen, Christ will come again' (*Eucharistic acclamation*, 1).

Hope protects us from discouragement, it preserves us from naive optimism, or undue pessimism, it keeps us orientated towards the true goal of our journey as the people of God - the coming of the Kingdom and the beatific vision of God.

Therefore, I want to ask each one of you who reads *Fit for Mission? Church*:

- Are you a person of hope?

- Have you cultivated the virtue of hope that you received at baptism?

- Do you pray for the virtue of hope?

- Have you hope enough to face with me the reality of our church fairly and squarely?

Pope Benedict XVI calls on all of us - but particularly young Catholics - to be 'ambassadors of hope' in a culture addicted to self-destructive sin. We must be living reminders that there is a genuine alternative to the pessimism and weariness of sin.

> You can convince them of the need to choose the path of life and shun the path of death, because you speak from experience. All through the Gospels, it was those who had taken wrong turnings who were particularly loved by Jesus, because once they recognised their mistake, they were all the more open to His healing message. (Pope Benedict XVI, World Youth Day 2008).

1.2 Fit for Mission? - A New Hope for our Church

As a result of the lengthy consultation we have undertaken in my diocese I have drawn a number of questions and conclusions from the wealth of information and responses that have been passed on to me from all 108 parishes in the diocese.

As the people of my diocese know, one passage of scripture has been our inspiration- the people of God *gathered* around Christ through His sacraments, to be empowered and *sent* out in His mission to the world:

> Then Jesus called the twelve together and gave them power and authority ... and He sent them out to proclaim the kingdom of God and to heal. (*Lk* 9:1-2).

As I commented in *Fit for Mission? A Guide*, Luke 9:1-2 tells us two key things about being the people of God:

1. **Gathered in the sacraments**: Jesus calls us together as His people to give us power and authority through His Word and Sacraments to serve the needs of others. He gathers us to heal us of the wounds of sin and to strengthen us in His Spirit.

2. **Sent out on a mission of hope**: Jesus sends us out as His people on a mission to proclaim the Kingdom of God and to bring 'light to those in darkness, those who dwell in the shadow of death, to guide us into the way of peace' (*Lk* 1:79).

Reflecting on scripture in the light of the snap shot of our parishes provided by the *Fit for Mission? Parish* review and the proposed reconfiguration of parishes, I draw the following conclusions about the reality of the Church as it presently appears in my own diocese, and I am sure, many other similar dioceses:

➤ The majority of our energy and charisms as the people of God are focused on being gathered through the sacraments. Lay liturgical ministries are well developed in most parishes, though there are exceptions. There is a good deal of collaboration between most clergy and laity in service of the liturgy.

➤ Though we are strengthened and healed by the Lord through His Word and Sacraments, the majority of us are not responding to Our Lord's call to go out on His mission of hope. In particular, mission in the parishes with families and young people are undeveloped or underdeveloped, with a few exceptions. (The Sacramental Priorities from the *Final Proposals* of the *Fit for Mission?* review conclude that it is important that parishes: 'Develop mission with families through relationships with primary schools' and 'Develop greater parish links and collaboration with secondary schools').

➤ The passion to serve the Lord is noticeably absent in many cases - there seems to be at times a tiredness and reticence to preach the gospel.

➤ One of the reasons why we are gathered but not sent is also due to a lack of confidence and knowledge of the Catholic faith. This results from a lack of ongoing formation and trained lay catechists. (The Sacramental Priorities from the *Final Proposals* of the *Fit for Mission?* review conclude that it is important that parishes: 'Develop ongoing formation encouraging lay leadership' and 'Establish faith sharing/ RCIA groups').

➤ As a consequence of being gathered but not sent, our Church often seems inward looking, self-involved and detached from the everyday life of our wider communities.

➢ It appears that many of us have forgotten the basic truth about the nature of the Church, that we have been gathered as the people of God not to be served but rather to serve God and each other, especially the weak and the poor.

I have sometimes noticed weariness, even hopelessness, among some clergy and laity, when asked to engage with the challenges that face us as the Church - sometimes this was reflected in the different levels of engagement with the entire *Fit for Mission?* process.

I understand some of the reasons for this, as I wrote in *Fit for Mission? A Guide*:

'I know how hard priests, deacons, religious and lay people have worked in living and proclaiming the Word of God, celebrating the sacraments and undertaking the ministry of charity, justice and peace. It is a hard thing to ask you to confront with me the situation facing our diocese, for sometimes it does feel that *'we worked hard all night long but have caught nothing!'*

Also, at times it would appear to me that we have talked too much and done too little.

> "Master, we worked hard all night long but have caught nothing, but if you say so, I will let down the nets". And when they had done this they netted such a huge number of fish that their nets were beginning to tear, so they signalled to their companions in the other boat to come and help them. (*Lk* 5:5-6).

St Peter's response, through the grace of truly hearing Christ's command, shows us the power and the promise of hope. A hope that will free us from our weariness, apathy and cynicism, *'At your word I will let down the nets!'* We too, like St Peter, must be willing to let down our nets in our own day.

1 Is our Church Alive with the Hope of Christ?	
Areas for reflection	**Suggested Actions**
<ul><li>When I think about the church, what questions are close to my heart?</li><li>Am I a person of hope?</li><li>Have I cultivated the virtue of hope that I received at baptism?</li><li>Do I pray for the virtue of hope?</li><li>Have I hope enough to face the reality of our church fairly and squarely?</li><li>Am I ready to go out and, like St Peter, 'let down my nets'?</li></ul>	<ul><li>Determine which area of the Church I am called by God to work in, where am I being sent to proclaim the kingdom of God?</li><li>Review my on-going formation.</li><li>Decide how I will ensure I am confident and knowledgeable in the Catholic faith.</li></ul>

2   The Second Vatican Council - The Light of Hope

For those of us who remember the experience of the Second Vatican Council, one of the graces received at that time was the conviction of great hope, of spirit-filled expectation of healing, renewal and growth. It was a time of exuberant confidence in the power of the Gospel to renew the face of the world.

It was as if we were in Galilee again during those heady days when the apostles walked with the Lord, hearing the liberating truth of His words and seeing His love, bringing miracles to all wounded by sin, sickness and doubt. And the world flocked to Him, knowing that He spoke with power and authority.

And the world flocked to Rome - through the media - during the Council, knowing that something wonderful was happening. Christ was speaking His words of hope and healing with authority to the peoples of our times. The 'new spring' so hoped for by Cardinal Newman seemed about to happen.

2.1   Are our Hearts and Minds open to Vatican II?

I know that some, looking back at the Council, have accused the Council Fathers of naive optimism and idealism concerning 'the world, the flesh and the devil'. But you just have to read through *Gaudium et Spes* (*GS*) to see the Council Fathers wise understanding of the anxiety and delusion in the world (*GS* 10), the power of sin (*GS* 13) and the combat with evil (*GS* 37). These prove that hope does not avoid hard truths, but sees them from the perspective of the Risen Lord (*GS* 22).

Others seek to dismiss the significance of the Second Vatican Council by saying it wasn't a 'dogmatic council', compared to the Council of Trent or Vatican I. Yes, Vatican II was different from all previous councils in that its documents contain no dogmatic definitions, disciplinary canons, or anathemas. However, this criticism ignores the fact that the Council sought to achieve something unique and irreplaceable in the history of councils - 'to show the strength and beauty of the doctrine of the faith.' (Pope John Paul II, *Fidei Depositum*).

I TELL YOU, YOU ARE PETER, AND ON THIS ROCK, I WILL BUILD MY CHURCH, AND THE GATES OF HADES WILL NOT PREVAIL AGAINST IT. I WILL GIVE YOU THE KEYS OF THE KINGDOM OF HEAVEN, AND WHATEVER YOU BIND ON EARTH WILL BE BOUND IN HEAVEN, AND WHATEVER YOU LOOSE ON EARTH WILL BE LOOSED IN HEAVEN."

MATTHEW 16:18–19

Finally, there is a tiny minority who remain distressed by the Second Vatican Council, as Yves Congar puts it, 'a sincere and faithful body of Catholics...attached to one form or another of the tradition of the Church' such as the Mass of St Pius V and the catechism of the Council of Trent'. However, I believe that though these are sacred and valuable expressions of Catholic tradition, they cannot put the living tradition of the Church into suspended animation! As well as cherishing all that is true and beautiful of the past, new ways of expressing the deposit of faith must be found to enable the Church to speak to the world of today.

2.2   The Holy Spirit inspired Vatican II

> But the Advocate, the Holy Spirit, whom the Father will send in my name, will teach you everything, and remind you of all that I have said to you. (*Jn* 14:26).

I am certain that, more often than not, when people criticise or seek to ignore the Second Vatican Council it is due to a lack of understanding of the authority of Ecumenical Councils in the life of the Church.

The Church holds that the teaching office of the Church [Magisterium], particularly through an Ecumenical Council, is assisted, helped and inspired by the Holy Spirit, who was promised and given to the Church so that it would be unfailingly faithful to the truth received from the apostles.

At the Second Vatican Council, 2,500 bishops gathered around Pope John XXIII and Pope Paul VI, to exercise the 'certain charism of truth' they had received from the Father, in the Son, through the Holy Spirit. (St Irenaeus, *Adversus Haereses* [*Against Heresies*], Book 4).

As Pope John Paul II puts it, based on his personal participation in the Council, 'The Council was a great experience of the Church; it was - as we said at the time - the "seminary of the Holy Spirit". At the Council the Holy Spirit spoke to the Church in all its universality, which was reflected in the presence of bishops from the whole world and by the presence of representatives of many non-Catholic Churches and communities'. (Pope John Paul II, *Crossing the Threshold of Hope*, p.159).

In the light of this, it seems obvious to me that the decrees of Vatican II and their post-conciliar development by the Magisterium are not to be treated as just one theological opinion among many, but must be seen as the 'authentic interpretation of the Word of God...entrusted to the living office of the Church alone'(*Dei Verbum* 10). As Fr Norman Tanner explains it, the doctrinal decrees of an Ecumenical Council have an 'absolute and timeless quality', which 'cannot be changed or rejected', though they are open to further development and clarification 'with regard to their expression'. (Norman Tanner, *The Councils of the Church: A Short History*, p. 5).

2.3   We are Living in the Time of the Council

> It is rare for a council not to be followed by much confusion. (Venerable John Henry Cardinal Newman, *Letter to the Duke of Norfolk*).

It strikes me that even though the Council closed 43 years ago we are still living in the time of the Council. What I mean by this is that - through the Holy Spirit - the Church is still growing through life-giving graces received at the Council. But it is not a painless growth. At times it would seem that graces are being obstructed and refused by some within the Church; that there is a failure to be loyal to the whole Spirit of the Council, where people choose only what appeals to them.

This begs the question, 'Why has the post-conciliar period been a time of both faithful implementation and brazen dissent in the life of the Church; a time of confidence and communion, but also of confusion and discord?'

Pope Benedict captures something of the confusion and discord in a passage from St Basil about the state of the Church after the Council of Nicea (325 AD):

> The raucous shouting of those who through disagreement rise up against one another, the incomprehensible chatter, the confused din of uninterrupted clamouring, has now filled almost the whole of the Church, falsifying through excess or failure the right doctrine of the faith... (St Basil, *De Spiritu Sancto*, XXX, 77; *PG* 32, 213 A; SCh 17 ff., p. 524).

2.4   A Time of Confidence and Communion

On the one hand, as a result of the Second Vatican Council we have witnessed a growth in confidence in the doctrine and life of the Church, under the pontificates of Pope Paul VI, Pope John Paul II and Pope Benedict XVI. Let me point out just a few of the most notable areas of growth and potential in the life of the Church over the past 40 years:

- ✓ This has been a time when many of the laity have stepped out of the pews to take a full and active part in the life of the Church, seen in their varied and active role in liturgy, leadership, catechesis and mission.

- ✓ There has been a great re-discovery of the bible throughout the Church, seen in catechesis, religious education, theology and the practice of *Lectio Divina*.

- ✓ There has been greater participation and thoughtful engagement in the liturgy, particularly in the celebration of the Mass, seen in such simple yet effective innovations as the Liturgy of the Word with children and the RCIA.

- ✓ There has been the renewal of the ancient grade of Holy Orders, the Permanent Diaconate, which has seen married and single men, bring their rich experience of work and family life into the hierarchy of the Church.

- ✓ There has been a rich and prophetic development of the social teaching of the Church, seen in the great teaching documents of Paul VI, John Paul II and

Benedict XVI - such as *Populorum progressio*, *Laborem exercens*, *Sollicitudo rei socialis*, *Centesimus annus* and *Deus Caritas Est*.

✓ In response to Paul VI's prophetic document *Humanae Vitae*, the Church has richly developed her doctrine on marital love, seen in Pope John Paul II's comprehensive theology of the body, the deepening understanding of marriage as a covenant and the *Billings Ovulation Method*, the *Creighton Fertilitycare Method* and the pioneering *NaProtechnology* medical programme.

✓ There has been a corresponding pace change in the Church's involvement in social justice and charity, seen in the work and advocacy of *CAFOD*, *Aid to the Church in Need*, *Cor Unum* and *Caritas*.

✓ There has been a renaissance in the Magisterium's guidance of the Church through three great publications that express the mind of the Second Vatican Council - The new *Code of Canon Law* (1983), the *Catechism of the Catholic Church* (1994), and the *Compendium of the Social Teaching of the Church* (2004).

✓ The growth of a theologically educated laity has been accepted as a beneficial development in the Church, especially through the work of Catholic institutes such as the Maryvale Institute etc.

✓ While the 19th century was the century of the new religious orders, the 20th century was the century of the New Movements in the Church, expressing the active role of the laity in seeking holiness and the guidance of the Holy Spirit, in communion with the Petrine Office, to bring about a New Pentecost in the Church.

✓ This has also been a springtime of the Holy Spirit in the life of the Church through the *Charismatic Renewal Movement* and associated groups, bringing a deep experience of prayer, praise and healing to countless people. It is hoped that the recent decline in the *Charismatic Movement* in this country will be reversed.

✓ The maturity of the Pope John Paul II generation will lead, I hope, to a resurgence of orthodox, committed adults in the Church, gradually renewing vocations to the priesthood, religious life and marriage.

✓ In many cases the older religious orders are returning to the charisms of their founding Fathers and Mothers, and increasingly offering to share their ways of life with lay people.

2.5   A Time of Confusion and Discord

On the other hand, in a misguided response to the Second Vatican Council we have witnessed a widespread dissemination of confusion and discord about doctrine and the discipline of the Church:

✗ A hundred thousand priests have left the practise of their priesthood.

✗ There has been a drastic decline in vocations to the priesthood and religious life in the West.

✗ There has been a steady decline in Mass attendance and participation in the sacrament of reconciliation.

✗ There have been abuses in the celebration of the Eucharist, that 'contribute to the obscuring of the Catholic faith concerning this wonderful sacrament'. (Pope John Paul II, *Redemptionis Sacramentum*, 6-9).

✗ There has been a marked increase in public expressions of dissent from the Church's doctrine and discipline in homilies, Catholic journals and theological works.

✗ It is not uncommon to come across clergy, religious and people who are disobedient to the Magisterium, particularly to the Pope.

✗ People are making important life decisions based purely on personal subjective judgements, detached from the teachings of the Church, Scripture and Tradition.

✗ There has been a steady decline in the number of Catholic marriages.

✗ There is a lack of generosity to the gift of life, seen in the delay in having families and the size of families.

✗ There is widespread confusion among Catholics about the values of fidelity and continence in marriage reflected in the divorce rate being equivalent to non-Catholic marriages.

✗ There has been the despicable crime of child sexual abuse, committed in families and by members of the Church.

✗ We are living through a period in the life of the Church when there has been a distortion of evangelisation and catechesis. This can be seen in the fragmentation in the transmission of the fullness of the faith, with omissions and neglect of some key truths, and an exaggeration of other aspects due to the misuse of experiential based catechesis.

✗ It has become somewhat commonplace to find the *Catechism of the Catholic Church* dismissed as a teaching resource in Catholic educational circles, seminaries and Catholic theological faculties.

Having listed the symptoms of confusion and discord I maintain it is important not to lose sight of the hope inspired by the Holy Spirit during the Second Vatican Council. As Pope Benedict reminds us:

Forty years after the Council, we can show that the positive is far greater and livelier than it appeared to be in the turbulent years around 1968. Today, we see that although the good seed developed slowly, it is nonetheless growing; and our deep gratitude for the work done by the Council is likewise growing. (Pope Benedict XVI, *Address to the Roman Curia offering them his Christmas greeting*, 2005).

2.6   Venerable John Henry Newman - Prophet of the Second Vatican Council

There are hopeful signs that Cardinal Newman's cause for beatification is advancing, particularly with the news that the Congregation for the Causes of Saints has requested that his body be exhumed from his grave and placed in the Birmingham Oratory.

Could this be a sign of God's providential care for His people in this country that now, in our hour of need, Cardinal Newman is, hopefully, to be raised to the altars of the Catholic Church? There are various reasons why I believe this to be the case:

I believe Cardinal Newman's renewed prominence will help us truly and fully implement the Second Vatican Council. He is, after all, recognised by many as the 'Father of the Second Vatican Council', particularly influencing the *Dogmatic Constitution on the Church*. (Ian Kerr).

Returning to Cardinal Newman's writings I also believe that he offers a prophetic vision of the times in which we live, seeing in embryo the social and political forces that are now growing against the practice of the Faith in this country.

For those who would accuse me of alarmism I would answer, how else can we view the closing of *Catholic* adoption agencies due to the Government's *Sexual Orientation Regulations*, or the growing intolerance towards Catholic schools witnessed by the establishment of a pressure group to agitate for the end of Faith Schools in any meaningful sense, or my own treatment for daring to promote the Catholic vision of education in my own diocese?

Cardinal Newman foresaw the rise of the secularising State with its marginalisation of Christianity in the name of 'tolerance' and so-called 'multi-culturalism'. He predicted the relentless drive to remove Christianity from the public arena, confining it to the private sphere. He accurately saw that the rejection of the Truth found in revelation would result in the nonsense of relativism.

He also foresaw the ascendancy of a secular ethic based purely on utilitarianism and statistics, which we increasingly see in healthcare in this country. He also accurately predicted the State enforcing its own version of morality that we see in political correctness.

Let me quote from the Cardinal's own prophetic words, which provide us with a powerful reading of the signs of the times:

> Is there not an opinion avowed and growing, that a nation has nothing to do with Religion; that it is merely a matter for each man's own conscience? - which is all one with saying that we may let the Truth fail from the earth without trying to continue it in and on after our time.
>
> Is there not a vigorous and united movement in all countries to cast down the Church of Christ from power and place? Is there not a feverish and ever-busy endeavour to get rid of the necessity of Religion in public transactions? ... an

> attempt to educate without Religion? - that is, by putting all forms of Religion together, which comes to the same thing; - an attempt to enforce temperance, and the virtues which flow from it, without Religion, by means of Societies which are built on mere principles of utility?
>
> An attempt to make *expedience*, and not *truth*, the end and the rule of measures of State and the enactments of Law? an attempt to make numbers, and not the Truth, the ground of maintaining, or not maintaining, this or that creed, as if we had any reason whatever in Scripture for thinking that the many will be in the right, and the few in the wrong?
>
> An attempt to deprive the Bible of its one meaning to the exclusion of all other, to make people think that it may have an hundred meanings all equally good, or, in other words, that it has no meaning at all, is a dead letter, and may be put aside?
>
> An attempt to supersede Religion altogether, as far as it is external or objective, as far as it is displayed in ordinances, or can be expressed by written words, - to confine it to our inward feelings, and thus, considering how variable, how evanescent our feelings are, an attempt, in fact, to destroy Religion? (John Henry Cardinal Newman, *The Patristical Idea of Antichrist*, Lecture 1).

I also believe that Cardinal Newman is a true example of Christian hope, seen as a realistic trust in the providential grace of God for His Church in our country. In his famous sermon 'The Second Spring' delivered to the First Provincial Council of Westminster in 1852, John Henry Newman looked forward to the re-established Catholic Church producing Doctors who will proclaim the Law of God, Preachers who call the country to penance and to justice, and Martyrs who shall 're-consecrate the soil to God'.

I am convinced that the Second Vatican Council is the Holy Spirit's answer to Cardinal Newman's hope for the Catholic Church in Great Britain. Once we fully embrace the true understanding and implementation of the Council, the charisms of the Holy Spirit will be poured upon us, producing the Doctors, Preachers and Martyrs needed for the challenges and trials of growth - the Second Spring:

> We know not what is before us, ere we win our own; we are engaged in a great, a joyful work, but in proportion to God's grace is the fury of His enemies. They have welcomed us as the lion greets his prey. Perhaps they may be familiarized in time with our appearance, but perhaps they may be irritated the more. To set up the Church again in England is too great an act to be done in a corner. We have had reason to expect that such a boon would not be given to us without a cross. It is not God's way that great blessings should descend without the sacrifice first of great sufferings. If the truth is to be spread to any wide extent among this people, how can we dream, how can we hope, that trial and trouble shall not accompany its going forth? (John Henry Cardinal Newman, *The Second Spring*, 1852).

2 The Second Vatican Council - The Light of Hope	
Areas for reflection	**Suggested Actions**
• How is the Holy Spirit asking me as a member of the Church to speak to the world of today? • What do I see as the signs of confidence and communion in the Church today? • What do I see as the signs of confusion and discord in the Church today?	• Consider reading / re-reading some of the prophetic teaching documents of Paul VI, John Paul II and Benedict XVI. These are available free on the internet at *www.vatican.va* • Consider the lay organisations available in my local area and whether the Holy Spirit is calling me to membership of one of these. • Pray for Cardinal Newman's cause, and consider reading and studying any of his works.

3   Handing on the Gift of the Council

The division and discord in the life of the Church is a source of pain and anxiety for many priests, deacons, religious and laity. Moreover it is harming our proclamation of Christ's life-giving Gospel and hindering the vigour and enthusiasm that it calls for.

One of the ways of discovering how to get our implementation of Vatican II right is to discern the ways members of the Church have got it wrong over the past 40 years! To do this I suggest we turn to the insights of the generation of Catholics actually involved in the proceedings of the Second Vatican Council. They provide a unique perspective on authentic implementation of the Ecumenical Council.

3.1   Eye witnesses to the Council

I am aware of the fact that, 40 years on, I am speaking to generations who have no recollection of the Council, even though their lives in the Church have been profoundly shaped by the Council. I am certain that in order to cut through 'the incomprehensible chatter, the confused din of uninterrupted clamouring' (St Basil), we need to hear from these witnesses of the true spirit and letter of the Second Vatican Council if we are to read the conciliar texts aright. The witnesses I will call upon were all participants in the Council: Henri Cardinal de Lubac; Bishop Christopher Butler; John Cardinal Heenan; Bishop Brian Foley; Pope John Paul II, and Pope Benedict XVI.

3.1.1   Henri Cardinal de Lubac SJ

Henri Cardinal de Lubac is regarded by many as one of the 'theological elders' of the Second Vatican Council, along with Fr Karl Rahner and Pope Benedict XVI.

He viewed Pope John XXIII's summoning of the Council as a prophetic act, seeking to guide the spiritual energies of the modern world and correct any deviations, through the 'inner renewal and rejuvenation of the whole Church'.

He came to the judgement that the Council documents show the 'wisdom, the balance and the profound sense of tradition which is inseparable from the boldness of the Pope's summons'.

However, writing in 1968, just 3 years after the close of the Second Vatican Council, he had already identified a widespread misinterpretation of the Council that threatened to distort its implementation. He passionately argued that if

Henri de Lubac SJ (1896-1991) was one of the Catholic theologians who made possible the Second Vatican Council. His work truly proved the worth of combining *ressourcement* [return to the sources of Catholic theology and life] with *aggiornamento* [bringing up to date, expressed through a critical and compassionate openness to the modern world]. He sought to release the energy and beauty of Patristic and Medieval theology and engage with the great social, political and cultural movements of the day.

He served as a consultant to the Preparatory Theological Commission for the Council, *peritus* [theological expert] to the Fathers, and a member of the Council's Theological Commission.

this distortion was not addressed as a matter of urgency by pastors and faithful in collaboration, the Council would be a 'complete failure'. (Henri de Lubac, *The Eternal Feminine*, p. 142).

With great perception and foresight, de Lubac very quickly saw that the misinterpretation of the Council that threatened the rejuvenation of the Church came from those who sought to break the balance between 'change and continuity'.

His reaction to those who mistakenly describe the Second Vatican Council as 'a rupture with the past' was to confidently state, 'I know only one Church, the Church of all time, the Church of Jesus Christ, the Church of the apostles'. (Henri de Lubac, *More Paradoxes*, p. 38).

De Lubac saw that to break the balance between change and continuity resulted in extremists promoting 'their own views rather than wholeheartedly adhering to the Council's decisions', with the goal of increasing the 'secularisation' of the Church in the name of 'radical transformation', 'pluralism' and the 'spirit of the Council'.

We have all witnessed with alarm many who profess to be Catholics disavowing the Church's teaching authority, particularly that of the Pope and the Congregation for the Doctrine of the Faith, dismissing apostolic traditions and the doctrines of the Fathers, and giving the place of honour to the fashionable opinions of society.

Henri de Lubac passionately argued that in order to truly implement the Second Vatican Council it is necessary for all of us to re-gain a Catholic sense of balance between change and continuity through maintaining the Catholic understanding of the Church, which in 'practise is a continuous tradition and a living, present authority'. (Henri de Lubac, *The Eternal Feminine*, p. 190).

➢ Following Henri de Lubac's insights into the implementation of the Council, here's a rule of thumb which I suggest can be applied to test if any proposed change in the Church is authentically Catholic - no change is authentically Catholic unless it fits into the continuity of tradition and meets with the agreement of the Magisterium of the Church.

➢ It is good to express this continuity of tradition through liturgy, art and music, while balancing this with openness to the inspiration of the new.

3.1.2   The English Witnesses to the Council - Butler, Heenan and Foley

3.1.2.1 Bishop Christopher Butler OSB

My second witness is Bishop Christopher Butler, the great English theologian of the Second Vatican Council.

Bishop Butler described Pope John XXIII as a 'teacher who loved the world,' who rejected the 'prophets of woe who tell us that our age is worse than former ones and behave as though they had learned nothing from history; yet history is the teacher of life'.

Bishop Butler saw the phrase 'aggiornamento in depth' as key to understanding the Council, which he defined as seeking new solutions that have a radical quality, entailing a 'searching discrimination between what is, after all, of the immutable essence of the Church, and all in her contingent existence that, however venerable, is yet - at least in principle - expendable'. (Bishop BC Butler, *Searchings*, p.258).

> **Christopher Butler** (1902-1986) attended the Council as President of the English Benedictine Congregation. During the Council he was appointed a member of the Theology Commission, assisted by Fr Karl Rahner. He emerged as one of the most significant prelates at the Council.

The motivation driving this *aggiornamento* in depth was to enable the Church to speak to modern man, to be a contemporary of modern man, so as to enter into dialogue. Bishop Butler saw it in terms of the Church adapting to the new environment brought about by modern progress.

He famously used the analogy of biological adaptation to a changing environment to describe the importance of the Council, identifying three possible ways for the Church to respond to change:

1. It can make itself plastic to the new situation, introducing change and modification within itself, while maintaining its basic identity intact.

2. It can refuse the challenge and entrench itself more firmly within its traditional structures.

3. It can flee from the challenge and take refuge on the borders of life, increasingly isolated and irrelevant.

Bishop Butler believed the third option was a very real peril for the Church:

> We have a guarantee from God that the Church will not cease to exist. We have no guarantee that it will not become so irrelevant to the human race that it survives...only on the margin of the real history of mankind. (Bishop BC Butler, *Searchings*, p.258).

> ➤ I conclude from this that the Church must not be introspective and ossified in the past, but must balance continuity with change through being - as Bishop Butler put it - 'an indomitable adventurer in new fields'. We must engage with the culture of our contemporaries, proclaiming the newness of Christ. In particular, we must be conversant and engaged with the new discoveries of science and technology. As Pope John Paul II exhorted us, each one of us must engage in the 'New Evangelisation.'

3.1.2.2 Cardinal John Heenan

My third witness to the Second Vatican Council is Cardinal John Heenan, whom I knew as a young priest.

John Heenan (1905-1975) attended all sessions of the Council becoming Archbishop of Westminster in 1963 and Cardinal in 1965. Cardinal Heenan also served on the special commission set up by Pope John XXIII to work on the draft decree on divine revelation.

Cardinal Heenan saw Pope John XXIII's passion for the Law as central to understanding his motivation for convening the Second Vatican Council. The Pope's first use of *aggiornamento* [bringing-up-to-date] - that key note of the Council - was associated with updating the Code of Canon Law.

According to Cardinal Heenan, Pope John XXIII was a 'priest of intense self-discipline and a great believer in law' which he knew as 'the surest safeguard of human liberty'.

Pope John saw the Council's success or otherwise in updating the Church's law as a test of 'the practical application of the provisions of ecclesiastical discipline' (Pope John XXIII, *Homily*, Conversion of St Paul, 25th January 1959).

Unfortunately for the reception of Vatican II, many Catholics have reacted against the idea of law, seeing it as restrictive instead of protective. Sadly, I have witnessed at first hand, in the state of the Church in this country, the anarchy and harm caused by this rejection of the rightful place of law in the life and liturgy of the Church.

In Cardinal Heenan's judgement the liberating reforms of the Council were given no real chance of being tested because Catholic rebels used the reforms to undermine authority and discipline in the Church. He characterised this as a sickness that had infected the body of the Church.

➢ I am convinced that we would all benefit from a deeper, more consistent adherence to the new *Code of Canon Law* (1983) and the revised *General Instruction of the Roman Missal* (2005). Both express - in a codified form - the great doctrinal and liturgical truths emphasised by the Second Vatican Council. If observed in our day-to-day life in parishes and the diocese, they are two important practical guarantees of the authentic implementation of the Council.

3.1.2.3 Bishop Brian Foley

My fourth witness to the Council is close to us in Lancaster, our own Brian Foley, my late predecessor as Bishop of Lancaster for 23 years, and, before he died, the last surviving English bishop who attended the Second Vatican Council.

Bishop Brian Foley was a steadfast defender of Pope John XXIII's intention that Vatican II should be a pastoral council, saying in his address to the Fathers in 1964:

'The purpose of the Council is a pastoral one. It is concerned with restoring religious practice to 'de-Christianised' parts of the world and with bringing the gospel to those who have not received it. Now, this object will not be achieved principally by a new liturgy or by new scriptural and doctrinal insights but rather by a truly pastoral apostolate. This is shown by the history of the Church and by present experience.' (Alberic Stacpoole, *Vatican II Revisited*, p. 258).

> **Brian Charles Foley** (1910-1999), consecrated Bishop of Lancaster in 1962, attended all four sessions of the Council. Bishop Foley spoke on the centrality of the priestly apostolate of the care of souls in building up the Church.

It seems to me that both Pope John XXIII and Bishop Foley saw the 'care of souls' as essential to the effectiveness of a 'pastoral' Council. Even during the proceedings of the Council, Bishop Foley voiced his concern that the 'liturgical and other reforms enacted by the Council will remain without effect...will not find fruition' if the priest's care of souls was not central to the vision of the Council. (Alberic Stacpoole, *Vatican II Revisited*, p. 263).

> ➤ It is clear that Bishop Foley was prophetic in his warning to the Council Fathers - the reforms enacted by the Council will not come to fruition if detached from the priests' care of souls. No amount of time spent in justice and peace work or liturgical reforms - though good in their rightful place - will compensate for priests getting to know families in their parishes.

> ➤ Therefore, if we would see the full implementation of the Council there needs to be a renewal of the 'care of souls' in our parishes. This in turn may help us to experience a reawakening in the ministry of promoting vocations. Granted that we may have fewer priests in the future, we must consider ways to remedy this lack in our lives.

3.1.3 Pope John Paul II

My fifth witness to the Council is that towering figure of 20th century Catholicism, Pope John Paul II.

Pope John Paul II explained that his primary task and definitive duty was to complete the implementation of the Second Vatican Council. He described the Council as 'an event of utmost importance in the almost two thousand year history of the Church'. (Pope John Paul II, *Crossing the Threshold of Hope*, p. 157).

I see the election of the first non Italian Pope in 455 years as a visible symbol of the true reforming spirit of the Second Vatican Council - change and continuity. There was so much that was new in the pontificate of Pope John Paul II, combined with a strong sense of Catholic identity founded on continuity with the truth of the past.

The reason why the Holy Father viewed the Second Vatican Council as an event of utmost importance and a 'great gift' was because Pope John XXIII gave it the purpose of showing 'the strength and beauty of the doctrine of the faith'. The Council's principal task was to guard and better present the 'precious deposit of Christian doctrine in order to make it more accessible'. (Pope John Paul II, Apostolic Constitution, *Fidei Depositum*).

He concludes that at the heart of the Second Vatican Council was the recognition that the world needs purification, needs conversion through men and women of today encountering Christ through the Church's presentation of the strength and beauty of the faith. (Pope John Paul II, Apostolic Letter, *Tertio Millennio Adveniente*, 18-19).

Like Henri de Lubac - his colleague on the *Gaudium et Spes* sub-commission - Pope John Paul II identified the correct interpretation of the Council as hinging on balancing change and continuity:

> In the history of the Church, the "old" and the "new" are always closely interwoven. The "new" grows out of the "old", and the "old" finds a fuller expression in the "new". Thus it was for the Second Vatican Council and for the activity of the Popes connected with the Council, starting with John XXIII, continuing with Paul VI and John Paul I, up to the present Pope. (Pope John Paul II, *Tertio Millennio Adveniente*, 18).

Pope John Paul II saw the new *Catechism* as an indispensable way in which 'all the richness of the teaching of the Church following the Second Vatican Council could be preserved in a new synthesis and be given a new direction.' (Pope John Paul II, *Crossing the Threshold of Hope*, p. 164).

The *Catechism's* goal of presenting an 'organic synthesis of Catholic doctrine' (*CCC* 11), in order to convey the 'melodious symphony of revealed truth' captures exactly the purpose of the Second Vatican Council. As Aidan Nichols puts it, the Council had the task of 'furnishing a doctrinal overview of Catholic teaching in its total harmony', in order to more effectively disclose 'the force, radiance and inspirational power of Christian truth in its plenary Catholic form'. (Aidan Nichols, *The Splendour of Doctrine*, p. 2).

Pope John Paul II (1920-2005) attended all sessions of the Second Vatican Council as bishop, and later as archbishop of Krakow. He addressed the Council debates on liturgical reform, revelation, religious freedom, the lay vocation, the Christian understanding of the world and the problem of atheism.

Pope John Paul II's greatest contribution to the work of the Council was as a member of the sub-commission tasked with preparing the final working draft of the Pastoral Constitution on the Church in the Modern World [*Gaudium et spes*]. He worked in one of the subgroups alongside some of the great theologians of the 20th century - Henri de Lubac, Yves Congar & Jean Danielou.

Pope John Paul II viewed *Gaudium et Spes* 22 as the theological linchpin of the entire council, 'It is only in the mystery of the Word made flesh that the mystery of man truly becomes clear' (George Weigel, *Witness to Hope*, p.169).

> The Spirit who spoke through the Second Vatican Council did not speak in vain. The experience of these years allows us to glimpse the possibility of a new openness towards God's truth, a truth the Church must preach "in season and out of season" (cf. 2 *Tm* 4:2). (Pope John Paul II, *Crossing the Threshold of Hope*, p. 165).

> ➤ Following Pope John Paul II's insight that the unique purpose of the Council was to guard and present better the doctrine of the faith through conveying its strength and beauty, I am now more convinced than ever that the *Catechism of the Catholic Church* must be at the centre of the life of every parish and school. If we seek to faithfully implement the Second Vatican Council, the *Catechism of the Catholic Church* is our indispensable guide and powerhouse of the Holy Spirit.

3.1.4 Pope Benedict XVI

And now we come to my final witness to the Council, our Holy Father, Pope Benedict XVI.

In his first message as Pope, he confirmed his determination to implement the Council, seeing it as both a ' "compass" by which to take our bearings in the vast ocean of the third millennium', and an 'authoritative rereading' of the Gospel applied to today's world.

However, Pope Benedict asks the urgent question - when we have gained so much that is positive from the Council why have there been such tragic and harmful loses occurring in the Church? What is causing this dissension and division in the communion of the Church?

Pope Benedict XVI locates the source of this failure in the implementation of the Council in the ascendancy of a misinterpretation, which he characterises as the 'hermeneutic [interpretation] of discontinuity'. The dissension results from the quarrel between those who see the Council as a break with the past and those who see the Council in continuity with the past the 'hermeneutic of continuity' (Pope Benedict XVI, *Address to the Roman Curia offering them his Christmas greeting*, 2005).

Pope Benedict XVI (1927-) attended all sessions of the Second Vatican Council as an official *peritus* [theological adviser] to Cardinal Frings, a highly influential figure in the Council. Though unable to address the bishops from the floor of the Council, Joseph Ratzinger - as he then was - advised all the German bishops, gave lectures on Council topics and worked with other influential *periti*, including Hans Küng and Karl Rahner.

He is credited with having a major hand in drafting the Council's highly regarded Dogmatic Decree on Revelation [*Dei Verbum*], and he wrote sections 22 and 23 of chapter 3 of *Lumen Gentium*, dealing with the role of Bishops and collegiality.

During the third session of the Council, he served on the editorial committee established to re-draft the decree on missionary activity, *Ad Gentes*.

3.2   Did We Break with the Past?

The misinterpretation that sees the Council as marking a definitive break with the past has its origins in a misunderstanding of the Church's relationship with her own history and her relationship with the world.

Misunderstanding the Church's connection with her own past, has led to a continual uncertainty and questioning about the identity of the Church. Even more damaging, it has led to a 'deep rift in her relationship to her own history, which seemed to be everywhere sullied'.

> It was precisely the break in historical consciousness, the self-tormenting rejection of the past that produced the concept of a zero hour in which everything would begin again... (Joseph Ratzinger, *Principles of Catholic Theology*, p. 372).

Regarding the Church's relationship with the world, Joseph Ratzinger argues that it became an 'almost painful willingness to take seriously the whole arsenal of complaints against the Church, to omit none of them.' This resulted in some seeking to learn from the world wherever possible, and to seek and to see only the 'good' that was promoted by the world.

These misinterpretations have led to the distortion of the Catholic identity of those in the Church who relentlessly criticise the Church's past, denigrate our Catholic heritage and advocate what the secular world holds up as 'good' - the promotion of rights detached from responsibilities, divorce, contraception, abortion, IVF, homosexual acts/unions and so-called 'safe-sex'.

The incorrect 'break with the past interpretation' takes its starting point in the last document formulated during the Council, *Gaudium et Spes*, with its impulse towards the new and its orientation to the modern world. Pope Benedict XVI comments that in this misunderstanding the other conciliar documents are dismissed as resulting from compromises with the past and not representing this 'new spirit'. Only the impulses towards the 'new' in the conciliar documents are incorrectly acknowledged as partaking in the 'spirit of the Council'.

> There is no "pre" or "post" -conciliar Church; there is but one, unique Church that walks the path toward the Lord, ever deepening and ever better understanding the treasures of faith that He Himself has entrusted to her. There are no leaps in this history, there are no fractures, and there is no break in continuity. In no wise did the Council intend to introduce a temporal dichotomy in the Church. (Joseph Ratzinger, *The Ratzinger Report*, p.35).

3.3   Embracing the New through being True to the Past

Pope Benedict XVI proposes that the authentic interpretation of the Council has been at work at the same time as the discord and confusion caused by the misinterpretation, one that, 'silently but more visibly, bore and is bearing fruit'.

He characterises the authentic interpretation as being one of continuity and renewal, which has its origins in Pope John XXIII's vision for his Council and Pope Paul VI's shepherding of the Council's immediate implementation.

Pope John XXIII was emphatic that the Council was to transmit 'doctrine, pure and integral, without any attenuation or distortion', the patrimony of 20 centuries.

He went on to make the famous distinction that was to guide the deliberations and expression of the Council: 'The substance of the ancient doctrine of the deposit of faith is one thing, and the way in which it is presented is another.'

In response to the growing confusion caused by those in the Church seeking to 'adopt an entirely new and unprecedented mode of existence', Pope Paul VI proposed an effective remedy,

' The Church must get a clearer idea of what it really is in the mind of Jesus Christ as recorded and preserved in Sacred Scripture and in Apostolic Tradition, and interpreted and explained by the tradition of the Church under the inspiration and guidance of the Holy Spirit.' (Pope Paul VI, *Ecclesiam Suam*, 26).

Pope Benedict expresses the key to the authentic implementation of the Council as 'innovation in continuity', a demanding synthesis of fidelity and dynamism:

> Certainly we cannot return to the past, nor have we any desire to do so. But we must be ready to reflect anew on that which, in the lapse of time, has remained the one constant. To seek it without distraction and to dare to accept, with joyful heart and without diminution, the foolishness of truth... (Joseph Ratzinger, *Principles of Catholic Theology*, p. 393).

The Holy Father concludes - and he is surely right - that wherever this correct interpretation has guided the implementation of the Council, 'new life developed and new fruit ripened.' This, too, is my experience as a pastor in the Church:

➤ Following Pope Benedict XVI's insight into the authentic interpretation of the Council being one of continuity and renewal, it is my earnest hope that every parish and every individual Catholic reads Scripture as interpreted and explained by the Tradition of the Church.

➤ Furthermore, I recommend that to coincide with the October 2008 Synod on 'The place of the Word of God in the Church', and, as part of our contribution to the Year of Paul, that study groups are set up to reflect on the Catholic understanding of the relationship between Scripture, Tradition and the Church's teaching authority as set out in the Dogmatic decree on revelation [*Dei Verbum*].

3.4   A Growth in Understanding

> For there is a growth in the understanding of the realities and the words which have been handed down. This happens through the contemplation and study made by believers, who treasure these things in their hearts (see *Lk*, 2:19, 51). (*Dei Verbum*, 8).

How are we to view the division in the Church between those who seek reform of the Church through breaking with the apostolic tradition and those who seek reform through continuity with the apostolic tradition?

When considering anything that is troubling or difficult I think it wise to turn to the life of Christ for enlightenment and guidance.

When we look at the Gospels we find that misinterpretations about the identity and role of Jesus were an ever present source of conflict and misunderstanding in Our Lord's life. After the feeding of the 5,000, the crowd wanted to 'take Him by force to make him king' (*Jn* 6:15).

Even the apostles often failed to understand Him and His role: 'Jesus said to them, "Why are you talking about having no bread? Do you still not perceive or understand? Are your hearts hardened?"' (*Mk* 8:17), ' "The Son of Man is to be betrayed into human hands, and they will kill him, and three days after being killed, he will rise again". But they did not understand what he was saying and were afraid to ask him' (*Mk* 9:31-32).

Those same apostles so misinterpreted the identity of Jesus that all of them deserted Him in the Garden of Gethsemane, and one of the Twelve betrayed Him into the hands of sinners.

I believe that since the Second Vatican Council we are almost divided into at least two groups:

❖   Those of us who are living the confusion of Gethsemane, trapped in misunderstanding and misinterpretation of the Council, running away into the darkness on our own, and

❖   Those of us who are open to the promise of Pentecost, gathered in prayer around Mary, Mother of the Church, Peter, the rock against whom the 'gates of hell will not prevail', and Paul, the apostle to the gentiles.

Mary, Peter and Paul are guarantors of continuity with the past and openness to the promise of the new. If we gather around them in prayer we can be sure of a new Pentecost in the Church. The sending of the Holy Spirit at Pentecost holds out the perennial hope to the Church 'that confusion and fear can be transformed into a vigorous conviction and sense of purpose'. (Pope Benedict XVI, World Youth Day 2008).

There are already intimations of the Holy Spirit's power and enlightenment throughout the people of God, particularly through new Ecclesial Movements throughout the world. I believe we need more prophets and visionaries rooted in the vision of Christ.

The Second Vatican Council's *Dogmatic Constitution on Revelation* [*Dei Verbum* (*DV*)] indicates authentic ways in which we can grow in understanding through the action of the Holy Spirit.

The teachings of the Church are not frozen in time or ossified like something dead, nor should we ever seek to turn the clock back. Rather, there is 'growth in understanding of the realities and the words which have been handed down' (*DV* 8). I think it important to notice two things here: first, the idea of 'growth', not 'revolution', or 'new beginning'; secondly, it is a growth in understanding of revelation received, 'handed down', not 'invented'.

The Council Fathers explain that this continuous growth in understanding of revelation in the Church occurs in two ways:

> ➤ Using the model of Mary in *Luke* 2:19, 51, 'who treasured all these things and pondered them in her heart', the Council Fathers state that growth in understanding in the Church is the responsibility of all believers who, through 'contemplation and study...treasure these things in their hearts through a penetrating understanding of the spiritual realities which they experience' (*DV* 8).

> ➤ The second way is 'through the preaching of those who have received through Episcopal succession the *sure* gift of truth'. During this time of confusion we can find reassurance in the fact that divine providence equips the Church with the 'sure gift of truth' through bishops in communion with the See of Rome.

'For as the centuries succeed one another, the Church constantly moves forward toward the fullness of divine truth until the words of God reach their complete fulfilment in her.' (*DV* 8).

3 Handing on the gift of the Council	
Areas for reflection	**Suggested Actions**
<ul><li>How do I meet the challenge of 'change and continuity'?</li><li>How do I ensure I am open to the life giving presence of the Holy Spirit?</li><li>Does practise in my parish adhere to the new *Code of Canon Law* (1983) and the revised *General Instruction of the Roman Missal* (2005)?</li><li>Is the focus of my parish on 'the care of souls'?</li><li>How can I help enable people today to encounter Christ through the Church's teaching of the faith?</li><li>Do I seek, through contemplation and study, to understand the spiritual reality of my life?</li><li>How do I avoid the temptation of setting up my own interpretation of the faith in opposition to the sure gift of truth in the Church?</li></ul>	<ul><li>Consider reading the introduction to the new *Code of Canon Law* (1983) available free on the internet at *www.vatican.va*</li><li>Commit to spending time each week exploring the *Catechism of the Catholic Church*, available free on the internet at *www.vatican.va*</li><li>Commit to spending time each week reading Scripture assisted by Catholic commentaries or groups which explore a correct interpretation in accord with the Tradition of the Church enlightened by the Holy Spirit.</li><li>During the month of October 2008 help operate a study group to reflect on the Catholic understanding of the relationship between Scripture, Tradition and the Church's teaching authority contained in *Dei Verbum*.</li><li>Review the arrangements for building up the community so that families in the parish get to know one another.</li></ul>

4   Have we forgotten what it is to be Catholic?

> But thanks be to God who always gives us in Christ a part in His triumphal procession, and through us is spreading everywhere the fragrance of the knowledge of Himself. To God we are the fragrance of Christ, both among those who are being saved and among those who are on the way to destruction...Who is equal to such a task? At least we do not adulterate the word of God, as so many do, but it is in all purity, as envoys and in God's presence, that we speak in Christ. (2 *Co* 2: 14-17).

Pope John Paul II once observed that the Catholic Churches in Europe were 'tempted to a dimming of hope', with Christians sharing in the bewilderment, disorientation, uncertainty and hopelessness of fellow Europeans. The Holy Father concluded that at the heart of this continental state of agitation and distress was a 'forgetfulness of God', through the promotion of a vision of man apart from God, apart from Christ. (Pope John Paul II, Post-Synodal Apostolic Exhortation, *Ecclesia in Europa*, 9).

I would also propose that for those within the Church who have not succumbed to a 'forgetfulness of God', some are at times showing signs of forgetfulness about being Catholic! As a bishop, observing this forgetfulness taking place among us has been a source of great sadness:

- Those who ignore their responsibility to God and neighbour forget they are Catholic.
- Those who deliberately miss Sunday Mass forget they are Catholic.
- Those who never pray forget they are Catholic.
- Those who deny they are sinners and avoid confession forget they are Catholic.
- Those who live oblivious to the suffering of the poor forget they are Catholic.
- Those who dissent from the authority of the Church forget they are Catholic.
- Those who use contraception, IVF and embryonic stem cell research forget they are Catholic.
- Those who use pornography forget they are Catholic.
- Those who have sex outside of marriage forget they are Catholic.
- Those who sexually abuse others, especially children and the vulnerable, forget they are Catholic.
- Those who commit homosexual acts forget they are Catholic.
- Those who commit domestic violence against their spouse or children forget they are Catholic.
- Those who help others take their own lives forget they are Catholic.
- Those who procure an abortion or assist another to have an abortion forget they are Catholic.

- Those who exploit their power and position forget they are Catholic.

- Those who physically or psychologically bully another forget they are Catholic.

- Those who cheat on benefits or taxes forget they are Catholic.

- Those employers who exploit their workforce forget they are Catholic.

- Those who have racist, sexist or homophobic attitudes forget they are Catholic.

4.1   Wake from the Forgetfulness of Sleep

> Besides this, you know what time it is, how it is now the moment for you to wake from sleep. For salvation is nearer to us now than when we became believers; the night is far gone, the day is near. Let us then lay aside the works of darkness and put on the armour of light; let us live honourably as in the day, not in revelling and drunkenness, not in debauchery and licentiousness, not in quarrelling and jealousy. (*Rm* 13:11-13).

I see this forgetfulness as just one more consequence of the genuine confusion deriving from the wide-spread misinterpretation of the Council. With so many dissenting voices challenging the authority of the Pope and bishops in communion with him, is it any wonder that many have forgotten what it means to be a Catholic?

I am convinced that if we are to wake from the weariness that is taking hold of the church in this country, we must return to the sources of our Catholic identity and mission, to renew our strength and vitality. In this way we will, through the grace of the Holy Spirit, be in a position to counter the negative and constraining influence of secularism and hedonism that is currently dominating our society.

The Father sent His Son to wake us from sleep, and longs to wake each one of us from the forgetful sleep of sin into the sun lit day of His forgiveness.

4.2   What does it mean to be Catholic?

> The Catholic Church is Jesus Christ spread abroad and communicated. (Henri de Lubac, *Catholicism*, p.48).

I think the first thing to acknowledge here is that nowadays people use the word 'Catholic' in many different ways. Some identify themselves as being Catholic through a grandparent or going to a Catholic school. Others identify themselves as being Catholic because they were baptised in the local Catholic Church and attend family christenings, weddings, and funerals. There are also those men and women who occasionally attend Mass at Christmas and/or Easter.

We must also mention the large number of Catholics who are divorced and re-married, who are unable to receive Holy Communion, but who faithfully attend Mass every Sunday. There are also the non Catholic husbands and wives of Catholic spouses who play an active part in the life of the parish, but who hold back from reception into the Church.

Faced with this complex reality, the following question begs an answer, 'what makes a person Catholic?'

The most useful place to begin answering this question is to explain one of the fundamental truths that make up the Catholic Church's understanding of herself - *All of humanity* is in a relationship with the Catholic Church, because she is the tangible expression [sacrament] in human history of Jesus Christ - God's desire and will to love and save the whole of humanity, embracing all cultures and races.

By this the Church means to teach two things:

1. All people, *without exception*, are called to participate in the Catholic unity of the People of God.

2. All people - from the Catholic faithful, other Christians, to the whole of humanity - either belong to the Catholic Church or 'are *related* to it in various ways'. (*Lumen Gentium* (*LG*) 13).

I understand this to mean all people are, to various degrees, in a relationship with the Catholic Church, either through some type of participation or connection with some aspect of our world view, beliefs or morality.

Our fundamental identity as the Catholic Church is to be inclusive not exclusive. This is why we welcome all people who turn up at our presbytery doors, attend our liturgies, or meet the criteria for admission to our schools. However, this does not mean that everyone who has some type of relationship with the Catholic Church *fully* belongs to the Catholic Church.

> The Church, the mystical body of Christ, is a communion which is at once inward and external, an inner communion of spiritual life (of faith, hope & charity) signified and engendered by an external communion in profession of faith, discipline and the sacramental life. (J Hamer, *The Church is a Communion*, p.93).

4.3 Who fully belongs to the Catholic Church?

The Council Fathers teach in their document *The Dogmatic Constitution on the Church [Lumen Gentium]*, that people fully belong to the Catholic Church through two inter-related levels of communion - invisible and visible. Both dimensions have to be present for someone to fully belong to the communion of the Church:

- The inner communion of faith, hope and love.

- The external communion of creed, liturgy and discipline.

4.3.1 Inner Communion of Faith, Hope and Love

First and foremost, we belong to the Church through 'possessing the Spirit of Christ' (*LG* 14). We must 'see through His eyes, love with his heart, share in His virtues' (*Fit for Mission? Schools*). We can only be incorporated into the Church through the special grace of Christ, not through our own merits or efforts.

The Council Fathers make it clear that if we do not respond to Christ's grace in thought, word and deed, not only will we not be saved, but we will be more severely judged:

> He is not saved, however, who, though part of the body of the Church, does not persevere in charity [love]. He remains indeed in the bosom of the Church, but, as it were, only in a "bodily" manner and not "in his heart". (*LG* 14).

In my experience, one of the most tragic things to witness as a pastor is to meet someone baptised into the 'life of Christ' who is eaten up with anger, resentment and animosity. Somewhere along the way they have lost touch with the Spirit of Christ and, forgetting how to love, they seem to have fallen out of love with the Church.

On the other hand, one of the greatest joys of being a pastor is to meet a person or a Eucharistic community animated by the spirit of Christ. There is a lightness of being, a generosity of Spirit, a readiness for genuine laughter, a willingness to take a lead, go the extra mile for anyone, or any cause. With such people the presence of love is tangible in the very air we breathe!

4.3.2   External Communion of Creed, Liturgy and Discipline

The word 'Catholic' is a combination of two Greek words *kath holou*, meaning 'universal', in the sense of 'together forms the totality' or 'completely whole'. As Hans urs von Balthasar puts it, 'Being Catholic means embracing everything, leaving nothing out'. (Hans urs von Balthasar, *In the Fullness of Faith*, p. 27).

The Church is Catholic because Jesus Christ is fully present in her, as St Ignatius of Antioch wrote on the way to martyrdom in Rome, 'Where there is Christ Jesus, there is the Catholic Church' (*CCC* 830). And as St Gregory of Nyssa puts it, 'He who beholds the Church really beholds Christ' (Henri de Lubac, *Catholicism*, p. 73).

Being 'Catholic' has the definite meaning of embracing the totality of Christ as He expresses Himself through His Catholic Church. The opposite of being Catholic would be to set ourselves as judges over the faith of the Church, to pick and choose what takes our fancy and reject what we dislike.

Simply put, the Church is Catholic because she receives from Christ, 'the fullness of the means of salvation' (*LG* 14) - Creed, Liturgy and Discipline. It is only through participating in this threefold visible bond willed by Christ that we can have the sure and certain knowledge, and experience, of being fully in union with Jesus Christ, and belonging to His Catholic Church. As Fr John Redford puts it, 'being a Catholic means accepting the whole of the means of salvation offered by Christ'. (Fr John Redford, *What is Catholicism?* p. 39).

4.4   Professing the Faith

At every baptism of a new member into the body of Christ the celebrant proclaims, "This is our faith. This is the faith of the Church. We are proud to profess it, in Christ Jesus our Lord." The Catholic Church teaches that there are two, inter-related aspects to this faith - there is the subjective, personal commitment to God, and there is also the objective, revealed truth believed in. This objective, revealed truth is not just intellectual and verbal, it is symbolic, it is sacramental, it is in fact the person of Jesus Christ.

Over the years since the Council I have increasingly observed a weakening in understanding among Catholics of these two, inter-related aspects of faith. Among some there has been the tendency to allow the subjective, personal experience of faith to override the objective, revealed truth of the Church.

As I wrote in *Fit for Mission? Schools*, this over emphasis on the subjective experience of faith as the primary criterion in professing the faith tends to make us the 'judges' of God's revelation in Christ, when in fact God's Word - expressed through the collective experience of the Church - should enlighten and explain the meaning of our personal faith. (*Fit for Mission? Schools*, p. 35).

DO NOT DOUBT BUT BELIEVE. THOMAS ANSWERED HIM, "MY LORD AND MY GOD!"

JOHN 20:27-28

The consequence of this ascendancy of a 'privatised' faith has been nothing short of the rejection of the 'Catholic' profession of faith by many who claim to be Catholics! One would have to add that we are living through a period in the life of the Church when there has been a fragmentation in the profession of the fullness of the faith, with omissions and neglect of some key truths and an exaggeration of other aspects.

As bishop, I should like to propose to you a number of ways to adhere to a truly Catholic profession of faith:

> A vital dimension of being Catholic is accepting the totality of the Church's doctrine. This is the only way of guaranteeing that Catholics are bound together 'as a whole'.

> Therefore, 'Catholic' refers to those who accept the universal faith of the Church, as opposed to those who accept only part of it.

> Communion with Rome is an essential part of Catholicity. One is a 'Catholic' who accepts the wholeness of the Christian faith as expressed in that fullness of communion with the Bishop of Rome, the Successor of Peter.

> The See of Rome, in communion with the whole Church, has articulated the full profession of faith through the *Catechism of the Catholic Church*, which 'aims at presenting an organic synthesis of the essential and fundamental contents of Catholic doctrine, as regards both faith and morals' (*CCC* 11).

4.5   Celebrating the Sacraments

At the heart of the Catholic understanding of the importance of sacraments is a fundamental truth about the Catholic Church - a sacrament cannot be self-administered, it can only be received as a gift. One cannot make the Church but only receive her. As Cardinal Ratzinger put it, the Church is an encounter with something not one's self.

In my ministry as priest and bishop, I have come across the following attitudes that fail to understand the Catholic vision of sacramental life:

- Catholics who say they don't need to participate at Mass on Sunday because they can just as well, or even better, pray at home.

- Catholics who protest that they don't need to go to confession because they can gain God's forgiveness in the privacy of their sitting room.

- Catholics who say a positive consequence of the decline in vocations to the priesthood is that soon we'll be able to have parishes just run by lay people, at long last rid of clericalism!

Such attitudes betray a failure to grasp the Catholic understanding that sacraments - the only objective way of encountering Christ - can only be received, in ordinary circumstances, from a Catholic ordained minister, or in the case of marriage in the presence of an ordained minister.

The Catholic understanding of sacraments as dependent on apostolic succession protects these precious encounters with Christ from subjective, personal whim or manipulation. To put it simply, the sacrament of Holy Orders guarantees the authentic 'handing on' of the *truth* of Christ in the other sacraments.

I suggest that the following elements are important for living a Catholic sacramental life:

- ➤ Hearing the Word of God as *proclaimed* in sacramental liturgy;

- ➤ Reading Scripture in the light of the Tradition and teaching of the Catholic Church, exemplified by the *Catechism of the Catholic Church*, so it can be properly understood;

- ➤ Appreciating the teachings of bishops, in genuine communion with the Pope;

- ➤ Participating regularly in the sacramental life of the Church, particularly Sunday Mass, and

- ➤ Constantly seeking ways of bringing liturgy and life closer together.

4.6   Recognising the Authority of the Pope and Bishops

Lumen Gentium makes it clear that the third bond necessary to fully belong to the Catholic communion is recognition of the government of the Church (*LG* 14). This is not the same thing as the relationship between the citizen and the political government of a country, because Catholics believe that Christ Himself is *active* in governing the Church through the Pope and bishops.

There is an important point that needs be made here - yes, the Church teaches that Christ is active in governing through the Pope and bishops, however, the Second Vatican Council made it clear that this does not mean an autocracy - absolute power in the hands of a few - but it means government through shared dialogue and leadership.

Those in hierarchical ministry - bishops, priests and deacons - are not to be understood as a separate clerical caste but remain part of the people of God:

> For the nurturing and constant growth of the People of God, Christ instituted in His Church a variety of ministries, which work for the good of the whole body. For those ministers who are endowed with sacred power are servants of their brethren, so that all who are of the People of God, and therefore enjoy a true Christian dignity, can work towards a common goal freely and in an orderly way, and arrive at salvation. (*LG* 18).

Therefore, the Pope and bishops are first and foremost servants of the people of God, who govern for the ultimate common good of the people, for our salvation.

Another key point to remember is that the laity - through baptism - participate in Christ's kingly office. Therefore, lay men and women have a duty based on knowledge, competence or outstanding ability to express their opinion on things which concern the good of the Church (*LG* 37) - as we have sought to encourage in the diocese of Lancaster through the *Fit for Mission?* initiative.

The Magisterium - as the other partner in the dialogue - has the duty to ascertain the sense of the faithful [*Sensus Fidelium*] 'with care to discriminate between views actually inspired by faith and mere opinions that could well be due to the influence of the secular climate'. (Avery Dulles, *The Craft of Theology*, p. 117).

> **'Sense of the Faithful'** [*Sensus Fidelium*]: The entire body of the faithful, anointed as they are by the Holy One, cannot err in matters of belief. They manifest this special property by means of the whole people's supernatural discernment in matters of faith when "from the Bishops down to the last of the lay faithful" they show universal agreement in matters of faith and morals. That discernment in matters of faith is aroused and sustained by the Spirit of truth. **It is exercised under the guidance of the sacred teaching authority**, in faithful and respectful obedience to which the people of God accepts that which is not just the word of men but truly the Word of God. Through it, the people of God adheres unwaveringly to the faith given once and for all to the saints, penetrates it more deeply with right thinking, and applies it more fully in its life. (*LG* 12).

Let's examine the essential relationship between governance in the Church, and a correct understanding of the *sensus fidelium*, by looking at two areas where recognition of the authority of the Pope and bishops appears to have fragmented in the lives of many Catholics.

4.7   Rich Christians in a Hungry World

The first area of breakdown is specific to Catholics in wealthy, western societies. I remember in the late 70's a book came out which caught the growing sense of prophetic outrage at the poverty in the developing world, it was called, *'Rich Christians in an Age of Hunger'*. The desire to bring real change to this situation came to a head with the famine in Ethiopia in the mid 80's, the Live Aid concerts and the Make Poverty History campaign. But has much real change been achieved?

Since the Second Vatican Council the Church had attempted to call attention to the growing suffering caused by poverty and lack of development in the so called 'Third World'. The sequence of teaching documents on social justice since *Gaudium et Spes* have attempted to convince Catholics that being active in the cause of social justice is as important to Catholic identity as weekly attendance at Sunday Mass.

However, the tragic truth is that looking around at our society, there appears in many cases to be nothing to distinguish Catholic families from other families in their pursuit of hedonistic materialism, with little regard for the suffering of the poor. For example, every year 10 million young children die of preventable diseases and malnutrition in developing countries.

The *sensus fidelium* is clear that wealthy Christians must act during an age of hunger, but this fact is ignored by many of us. As Pope Benedict XVI said in a recent address, 'the prevalent hedonistic and consumeristic mindset fosters in the faithful and in Pastors a tendency to superficiality and selfishness that is harmful to ecclesial life'. (*Address of his holiness Pope Benedict XVI to participants in the plenary assembly of the Pontifical Assembly of the Pontifical Council for Culture*. 8th March, 2008).

This wide-spread failure to take action to remove the causes of poverty in the developing world, ignores the three elements of an authentic Catholic *sensus fidelium*:

➢ Firstly, the Word of God makes it clear that God is on the side of those suffering injustice and poverty, and that God's judgement is against the religious rich who benefit from the inequality (cf. *The Book of Amos*).

➢ Secondly, the tradition of the saints consistently shows an active concern for social justice and care of the poor, exemplified by St Francis of Assisi, Blessed Mother Teresa of Calcutta, and so many others.

➢ Thirdly, all the modern Popes have insistently exhorted us to make social justice a defining characteristic of being Catholic. Pope Paul VI, in his prophetic encyclical *Populorum progressio*, pointed to the basic inequality at the heart of this injustice, 'the prevailing economic system if left to itself simply serves to 'widen the differences in the world's levels of life...rich peoples enjoy rapid growth whereas the poor develop slowly'. (Paul VI, *Populorum progressio*, 8).

4.8 Fully Embracing Life

The second area of breakdown that I am compelled to write about is in the use of contraception to regulate the number of children.

I have heard it expressed many times that the obvious rejection of the Church's teaching on contraception by many Catholic couples is an apparent expression of the *sensus fidelium* and, consequently the Church should drop its opposition to it and adopt a more permissive attitude.

This mistaken reasoning forgets three elements essential to the authentic *sensus fidelium*:

➤ Firstly, the *sense of the faith* must be founded on the Word of God and not secular opinion. Scripture is clear that there is an inseparable bond between sexual love, procreation and God's creative power and lordship over life.

➤ Secondly, the *sense of the faith* must cling to the faith held by the saints. The tradition of the Church has been consistently against contraception, be it *coitus interruptus*, condoms or the contraceptive pill.

➤ Thirdly, the *sense of the faith* must take its lead from the sacred teaching authority of the Pope and bishops. The Church does not take an opinion poll to ascertain the truth, but safe-guards the truth through the teaching office of the Pope. All Popes of the modern era have consistently taught - according to Scripture and tradition - that recourse to contraception is gravely wrong.

The main idea behind the *sensus fidelium* is not, therefore, to change the teachings of the Church - Christ's teachings - according to public opinion, but rather it is about the fact that it is God's will that all the people of God have the responsibility of preserving and maintaining the faith out of a sense of service towards mankind. We can only receive and embrace this faith, we cannot change it. It is a treasure entrusted to us, which we must guard loyally. (Herbert Vorgrimler, *Commentary on the Documents of Vatican II*, Vol. 1, p. 165).

4.9 The Battleground of Conscience

Since the Second Vatican Council, many people have justified their dissent from the doctrines of the Catholic Church, particularly sexual morality, by appealing to the duty to follow one's conscience, often claiming a conciliar mandate for 'loyal dissent' from a misreading of the *Declaration on Religious Liberty* [*Dignitatis humanae*].

Catholics who dissent from the teachings of the Church demand - in the light of their misreading of Vatican II - that we 'respect their consciences', meaning that we must hold that their subjective judgement of moral truth is equal to the objective divine truth preserved by the Church. While respecting their freedom of conscience, we cannot - in charity - respect their errors.

As Archbishop Charles Chaput writes in his excellent book, *Render unto Caesar* :

> Yet the Catholic faith does not hold, and Vatican II did not teach, that respect for conscience means that individuals have absolute sovereignty in determining their own truth, or that anyone's choice of beliefs is as good as any other. Even the secular order admits that some choices are good and others bad. Whatever we may tolerate, every person has duties to seek and serve the truth. (Archbishop Charles Chaput, *Render unto Caesar*, p. 129).

What is conscience? Many think conscience is purely a feeling, so we often hear the following self-justification, "If it feels alright, and it doesn't harm anyone else, then it's OK to do it". It is true that feelings are involved to an extent in following one's conscience, such as feelings of guilt, shame, or joy at seeing the good, but they are not the primary acts of conscience.

The Church teaches that conscience is a judgement of reason whereby we recognise the moral truth or worth of an act and it enables us to perceive and recognize a pre-existing divine law (*CCC* 1778). The important thing to grasp here is that conscience is an individual's *judgement*, and as such any of us can make the wrong judgement if we only rely on our feelings or instincts. Feelings are often self-serving and can easily be disordered.

One of the greatest errors of the current age is to hold that an individual's conscience is an infallible and autonomous guide to moral action. We have lost the sense that conscience, particularly one damaged by habitual sin, can make profoundly erroneous judgements.

The Church teaches that all of us are vulnerable to making erroneous judgements of conscience, if we are ignorant of natural law or divine law. (*CCC* 1792). Sources of ignorance include:

- Ignorance of Christ and his Gospel.

- Bad example given by others.

- Enslavement to one's passions.

- Assertion of a mistaken notion of the autonomy of conscience.

- Rejection of the Church's authority and her teaching.

- Lack of conversion and of charity.

Aware of our predisposition to make erroneous judgements of conscience, I sincerely believe that the best option available to us when we are considering whether to act against the teaching of the Church or not, is to always assume that the Church is right, and that I am wrong. Let's be clear here, I'm not advocating blind obedience, but the serious obligation to inform and educate our consciences with the doctrines of the Church (cf. *CCC* 1783-1785).

> People often face difficult issues in daily life. Some Catholics may find themselves sincerely unable, in conscience, to accept a point of Catholic teaching. When that happens, the test of a believer's honesty is his humility; that is, his willingness to put the matter to real prayer and the seriousness of his effort to accept the wisdom of the church and follow her guidance. If after this effort he still cannot reconcile himself with the teaching of the Church, he must do what he believes to be right, because ultimately every Catholic must follow his or her conscience. (Archbishop Charles Chaput, *Render unto Caesar*, p. 149).

What is not acceptable is for Catholics who cannot in conscience accept a particular doctrine of the Church to lobby and attack the Church, as if their subjective judgement is superior to that of the Magisterium.

4.10 The Dialogue of Obedience

> Though he was in the form of God, Jesus did not regard equality with God as something to be exploited, but emptied himself, taking the form of a slave, being born in human likeness. And being found in human form, he humbled himself and became obedient to the point of death - even death on a cross...
>
> ... Therefore, my beloved, just as you have always obeyed me, not only in my presence, but much more now in my absence, work out your own salvation with fear and trembling; for it is God who is at work in you, enabling you both to will and to work for his good pleasure. (*Ph* 2:6-8, 12-15).

So, what is the authentic Catholic relationship between the individual and the authority of the Pope and bishops?

Lumen Gentium 37 makes it clear that both the laity and pastors participate in Christ's spirit of obedience to the truth given Him by the Father. It was Christ's obedience to the will of the Father that gained us our redemption through His acceptance of the cost of divine love nailed on the Cross.

Therefore, being disciples of Christ we are all are bound to obey the Word of God contained in Scripture and Tradition. Christ is active in governing the Church through the Pope and bishops because they are obedient to the Word of God. They obey the Lord Himself. And lay men and women are called to co-operate with the Pope and bishops, who have been appointed by God as teachers and rulers:

> With ready Christian obedience, laity as well as all disciples of Christ should accept whatever their sacred pastors, as representatives of Christ, decree in their role as teachers and rulers in the Church. Let the laity follow the example of Christ, who, by His obedience even at the cost of death, opened to all men the blessed way to the liberty of the children of God. (*LG* 37).

"ABBA, FATHER, FOR YOU ALL THINGS ARE POSSIBLE; REMOVE THIS CUP FROM ME; YET, NOT WHAT I WANT, BUT WHAT YOU WANT."

MARK 14:36

At the heart of the Christian understanding of obedience is the imperative to empty oneself through a readiness to surrender to God's love (cf. *Jn* 14:15). This spirit of genuine humility is a prerequisite for all the people of God - bishops, priests, deacons, religious, lay women and men.

Cardinal Dulles is right when he comments that it is the painful duty of the Pope and bishops to set limits to what may be held and taught in the Church. Often the doctrine of the Church - such as its teaching on contraception - is not pleasing or acceptable to the general public (Avery Dulles, *The Craft of Theology*, p. 118). Like our Master before us, we sometimes have to speak hard truths to safe-guard God's word entrusted to us, and to protect the dignity of humanity. In season, or out of season, the one thing we must do is preach the word of life (2 *Tm* 4:2).

When I examine my post bag, it often seems to me that many Catholics think they have the right to pick and choose what statements or documents from the Holy See they will take seriously or ignore. As a priest of the diocese puts it, 'it's as if there are one billion Popes in the Church'. For all right thinking Catholics, this cannot be an acceptable state of affairs.

4 Have we forgotten what it is to be Catholic?	
Areas for reflection	**Suggested Actions**
• How do I fulfil my responsibility to God and to my Neighbour? • How do I ensure that I do not forget that I am a Catholic? How do I actively live my life so I am mindful of the joy and responsibility I have as a Catholic? • How do I return to the sources of our Catholic identity and mission, to renew my strength and vitality? • Do I have a lightness of being, a generosity of Spirit, a readiness for genuine laughter, a willingness to go the extra mile for anyone, or any cause? • Do I remain in the presence of love? • How do I ensure I appreciate the totality of the doctrine of the Catholic Church? • Do I participate in Christ's spirit of obedience to the truth given Him by the Father? • Do I have a Catholic understanding of conscience?	• Review your participation in the sacraments and identify if there are any areas in which you can deepen your encounter with the life giving Christ. • Review how you promote social justice and identify any additional actions you can take. • Review how you promote the Church's teaching on marriage's openness to life.

5   The Church is the Work of the Holy Trinity

> The Church shines forth as "a people made one with the unity of the Father, the Son and the Holy Spirit". (St Cyprian, quoted in *Lumen Gentium*, 4)

With all this talk about the business of governing the Church and the responsibilities of the faithful it's easy to start thinking that the Church is the work of human beings. From this thought, it's an easy next step to accept the *relativist a priori* that all religions are the works of human beings. This would be a mistake.

The Second Vatican Council starts from the revelation that the Church is a 'mystery' - the dwelling, expression and fruit of God, Father, Son and Holy Spirit, among humankind:

> The liturgy daily builds up those who are in the Church, making of them a holy temple of the Lord, a dwelling-place for God in the Spirit, to the mature measure of the fullness of Christ. (*Sacrosanctum Concilium*, 2).

When we talk of the Church we must not forget that we are dealing with the profoundest of mysteries - the self-giving love that is the Holy Trinity. This self-giving love has manifested itself in the salvation history of Israel, the incarnation of the Son of God and in His continual self-gift through time and space in His Church.

Therefore, the Holy Trinity is foundational to our understanding of the nature and role of the Catholic Church.

I think Pope Paul VI was right when he said that if we would revitalise the Church in herself we need to probe more 'deeply still the mystery, the plan and the presence of God above and within'. This faith is the secret to our confidence, our wisdom and that love which impels us to sing without ceasing the praises of God.

It is for this reason that I believe it imperative that we regain the sense of the origin of the Church in the life of the Holy Trinity. To put it simply, singing the praises of God is the reason of being for the Church. '*Cantare amantis est*' [Song is the expression of a lover]. (*St Augustine*).

5.1   God is One

The Council Fathers begin their document on Christian unity through establishing the Trinitarian source of the Church: The Church is one because the source of her unity is 'in the Trinity of Persons, of one God, the Father and the Son in the Holy Spirit' (*Unitatis redintegratio*, 2). The Council makes it clear that the Church is not a society created by humankind, but rather a communion brought about by God.

> What an astonishing mystery! There is one Father of the universe, one Logos of the universe, and also one Holy Spirit, everywhere one and the same; there is also one virgin become mother, and I should like to call her "Church". (St Clement of Alexandria CCC 813).

5.2   God is Three

The *Dogmatic Constitution on the Church* [*Lumen Gentium*] seeks for the foundation of the Church in the mystery of the triune God, explaining how the Church is related to each of the Divine Persons.

5.3   God the Father

Ultimately, the Church has her origins in the creative and salvific will of God - in the mission of God. *Lumen Gentium* 2 teaches that the Church is shaped by the self-giving grace of God poured out in creation and salvation history, 'already from the beginning of the world the foreshadowing of the Church took place' (*LG* 2).

> The eternal Father, in accordance with the utterly gratuitous and mysterious design of His wisdom and goodness, created the whole universe, and chose to raise up people to share in His own divine life... (*LG* 2).

The history of God's election and covenantal relationship with Israel is the story of the creation of His 'community of salvation', that was to become the Church of Christ.

I conclude from this the following practical implications for our lives as Catholics:

- ✓ As a Church we need to cultivate a greater and deeper appreciation of God's creation through dialogue with the natural sciences and the arts. We would do well to remember that wonder at the natural world is often the first step to faith.

- ✓ We need to spend more time contemplating the beauty and wonder of nature. Consequently, we must be increasingly involved with others in conserving and protecting the environment of our natural habitats.

- ✓ The history of Israel is also our history as a people, which means in practical terms that the Bible must be a vital force in the life of each parish and each individual Catholic if we are to gain an ever deeper knowledge of who we are as people chosen to share the life of God.

5.4   God the Son

The Son of God, before the foundation of the world, was destined to be sent by the Father into the world so that humankind could share in the life and friendship of the Holy Trinity. It is divine love not human sinfulness that determines the self-gift of the incarnation. The nature of Christ's mission was conditioned by, but was not determined by, man's need for salvation from His tragic sinfulness.

The Church is the Sacrament of the Incarnation, re-presenting the divine and human natures of Christ in the world. As such the Church makes present the reality of the incarnation, death and resurrection of the Son of God through word and deeds, through the proclamation of the Gospel and the celebration of the sacraments.

Lumen Gentium 3 conveys the essential truth about the Church that wherever Christ is present, there the reign of God is in action. This is key - the kingdom of God is not a place or thing, it is the co-operative action of God and individuals, loving, healing, forgiving, praying, praising and hoping. The reign of God is not a noun, it is a verb!

The foundational actions of the reign of God - Christ's sacrifice on the Cross made present in the sacrament of the Eucharist - constitute the presence of the Church among people. Again, it is important to point out that the Church - the mysterious presence of the reign of God - is a gift from on high, not a product of our minds or endeavours, even the most worthy.

I conclude from this the following practical implications for our lives as Catholics:

✓ One of the great treasures of Catholic spirituality is our tradition of the celebration of Mass and Eucharistic devotion, which is both profoundly Trinitarian and Christological. I encourage all of you to promote devotion to, and adoration of, the Blessed Sacrament. I know this will have a profound effect on the life of the parish in terms of its orientation and fruit, such as promoting a ministry for promoting vocations. (A Sacramental Priority in the *Final Proposals* of the *Fit for Mission? Parish* review).

> The Church, or, in other words, the kingdom of Christ now present in mystery, grows visibly in the world through the power of God... As often as the sacrifice of the cross in which "Christ, our Passover, has been sacrificed" (1 *Co* 5:7) is celebrated on an altar, the work of our redemption is carried on. (*LG* 3).

5.5 God the Holy Spirit

Pentecost is the moment when God's plan to share the divine life, love and friendship of the Holy Trinity with humankind was realised in time and space, in an upper room in Jerusalem, among the apostles gathered around Mary and Peter. Pentecost and the paschal mystery of Christ are the same event of self-giving love, involving the actions of two divine persons, the Son and the Holy Spirit, at one with the Father.

It is through the gift of the Holy Spirit that each one of us has 'access to the Father through Christ in the one Spirit' (*LG* 4). The Holy Spirit gives us many gifts essential to the life of the Church, but none more so than the 'unity of fellowship and service' which is a participation in the *communio* [union] at the heart of the Trinity of divine persons, one God. As Jesus prayed in his priestly prayer given to us in John's gospel,

> May they all be one, just as, Father, you are in me and I am in you, so that they also may be in us, so that the world may believe it was you who sent me. (*Jn* 17:21).

As unity is the characteristic of the Holy Trinity, then unity between believers should be the major sign of fully sharing in the life of God, as is His purpose and plan for His Church. *Lumen Gentium* 4 identifies two ways that the Holy Spirit creates this unity in the Church - 'He furnishes and directs her with various gifts, both hierarchical and charismatic, and adorns her with the fruits of His grace' (*LG* 4).

The key insight here is that the Council Fathers see the hierarchical and charismatic as complementary dimensions of the Church, deriving from one source, the Holy Spirit. Each dimension needs the other for the fruition of His grace in the life of the Church. However, I sometimes hear Catholics who are involved in the charismatic movement express impatience, even dissent, about some aspect of the hierarchical church to the point where they consider breaking away from the Catholic Church. This would never be the will of the Holy Spirit.

I strongly believe that our attitude towards the hierarchical Church will be transformed if we see it not as the human exercise of power but as an expression of the unifying activity of the Holy Spirit. Pope Benedict XVI had some important things to say about the Holy Spirit during World Youth Day in Australia in 2008. Reflecting on the theology of St Augustine, the Holy Father said:

> ...his experience of the love of God present in the Church led him to investigate its source in the life of the Triune God. This led him to three particular insights about the Holy Spirit as the bond of unity within the Blessed Trinity: unity as communion, unity as abiding love and unity as giving and gift... In a world where both individuals and communities often suffer from an absence of unity or cohesion, these insights help us remain attuned to the Spirit and to extend and clarify the scope of our witness. (Pope Benedict XVI, World Youth Day 2008).

I conclude from this the following practical implications for our lives as Catholics:

- ✓ *Lumen Gentium* 4 contains a very important truth for our Church in this current age of discord and disunity- if we are to enjoy the blessings of sharing the life of God through His Church allegiance and loyalty to the Successor of St Peter in communion with his brother bishops - as the unitive figure of the hierarchical Church - is essential for each one of us. The hierarchy is just as much a gift of the Holy Spirit as the charismatic gifts of prophecy, praise, healing or speaking in tongues.

- ✓ The Holy Spirit enables us to speak with one voice with a deep sense of unity, which is an urgent need of the time.

5 The Church is the Work of the Holy Trinity	
Areas for reflection	**Suggested Actions**
• How do I experience the Church as reflecting the Trinitarian nature of God?	• Make time to contemplate the beauty and wonder of nature. Review the ways in which you help conserve and protect our natural habitats. • Daily pray for the Pope and bishops and for the unity of the Catholic Church.

6   How do we Read the Documents of Vatican II?

Forty years after the close of the Second Vatican Council, how many of us frequently return to these wonderful documents for inspiration or to refresh ourselves about what the texts actually say? I am convinced that this is what we must do, because the Holy Spirit speaks urgently to us through the pages of the Council documents.

It can be a daunting thing to pick up a copy of Abbott's or Flannery's translations, and start reading the dense paragraphs, knowing that each word and phrase has been closely argued before agreement was reached for its inclusion in the final text.

Is there a key to unlock the 4 Constitutions, 9 Decrees and 3 Declarations, 103,014 words, and 992 footnotes of the Second Vatican Council?

6.1   The Four Keys to Unlocking the Council

The Final Report of the Extraordinary Synod of Bishops (1985) convened to celebrate the 20th anniversary of the close of the Council identified a number of principles to guarantee the authentic interpretation and implementation of the Vatican II documents.

One of the principles is that there will be a more profound acceptance of the Council if its four constitutions are seen as the keys to the other documents. (*Final Report*, 5).

Cardinal Ratzinger points out that the order in which the first two Constitutions were issued by the Council indicates the basic orientation of the whole Council's structure.

The Constitution on Sacred Liturgy was the first text issued, because 'worship, adoration, comes first. And thus God does'. He concludes that the Second Vatican Council intended to 'subordinate what it said about the Church to what it said about God and to set it in that context'. (Joseph Ratzinger, *Pilgrim Fellowship of Faith*, p. 125-126).

I think Cardinal Ratzinger is correct in highlighting that the Council sought to give primacy to God in its proceedings, and not primacy to man (as many popular interpretations have sought to argue through giving emphasis to the novelty of the pastoral constitution on the modern world [*Gaudium et Spes*]).

The four keys to Vatican II are divided into two groups that reflect Jesus' dual commandment of love - love of God and love of man:

Love of God

The First Key: *The Constitution on the Sacred Liturgy - Sacrosanctum Concilium*
Our love of God is expressed through the fundamental primacy we give to the praise and adoration of His divine love.

The Second Key: *The Dogmatic Constitution on Divine Revelation - Dei Verbum*
The Word of God, proclaimed in liturgy, gathers the Church together and calls for our response of love.

Love of Man

The Third Key: *The Dogmatic Constitution on the Church - Lumen Gentium*

The Church derives from the praise and adoration of God. The proclamation and generous distribution of the incarnate Word, through Gospel and Eucharist, manifests our co-operation with God's love for all humankind.

The Fourth Key: *The Pastoral Constitution on the Church in the Modern World - Gaudium et Spes*

The Church carries the light of love received from God out into the world, taking it into all the dark places of injustice and suffering in the knowledge that the light came into the world and darkness could not overcome it.

6.2 Other Principles to Interpret Vatican II.

The Extraordinary Synod indentified 5 other principles to authentically interpret the documents of Vatican II (*Final Report*, 5):

- ➤ Individual documents and passages should be read in light of the whole canon of Vatican II's Constitutions, Decrees and Declarations, so that the integral meaning of the whole Council is maintained.

- ➤ It is inauthentic to make a false distinction between the pastoral character of the Council and its doctrinal content.

- ➤ It is inauthentic to separate the spirit from the letter of the Council.

- ➤ 'The Church is one and the same in all Councils'. There should be more understanding of Vatican II's continuity with the great tradition of the Church.

- ➤ Vatican II speaks to the problems that we face today as a Church. It hasn't been superseded by events.

6 How do we read the documents of Vatican II?	
Areas for reflection	**Suggested Actions**
• When did I last read any of the 4 constitutions of Vatican II?	• Obtain copies of the four constitutions of Vatican II. These are available free on the internet at *www.vatican.va*

7   Key One: The Constitution on the Sacred Liturgy

"I HAVE EAGERLY DESIRED TO EAT THIS PASSOVER WITH YOU BEFORE I SUFFER, FOR I TELL YOU, I WILL NOT EAT IT UNTIL IT IS FULFILLED IN THE KINGDOM OF GOD."
LUKE 22:15-16

KEY ONE:

THE CONSTITUTION ON THE SACRED LITURGY

> **Sacred Liturgy.** Our love of God is expressed through the fundamental primacy we give to the praise and adoration of His divine love.

Of all the documents of the Second Vatican Council, the *Constitution on Sacred Liturgy*, *Sacrosanctum Concilium*, initiated some of the most visible and dramatic changes to the lives of Catholics. The constitution illustrates the authentic spirit of Vatican II, identified by Cardinal Henri de Lubac, as seeking to balance continuity with change.

Pope Benedict XVI captures this purpose of *Sacrosanctum Concilium* well when he writes in *Summorum Pontificum*, 'In more recent times, Vatican Council II expressed a desire that the respectful reverence due to divine worship should be renewed and adapted to the needs of our time'.

Liturgy is the wellspring of the life of the Church. It is the true centre and deepest mission of the Church - the adoration of the triune God. As such, it is the authentic *starting point* of all renewal.

> Only if man, every man, stands before the face of God and is answerable to Him, can man be secure in his dignity as a human being. Concern for the proper form of worship, therefore, is not peripheral but central to our concern for man himself. (Cardinal Ratzinger, *The Feast of Faith*, p.7).

7.1   Balancing Continuity and Change in the Liturgy

I think all fair minded people will agree that *Sacrosanctum Concilium* has succeeded in achieving a much needed renewal of the liturgy, in both the celebration of the sacrifice of the Mass and the sacraments. These achievements include:

❖ The active participation of the congregation, replacing the focus on the isolated priest celebrant, particularly expressed through the widespread practise of communion under both kinds, the re-introduction of the prayers of the faithful and the diversity of lay liturgical roles (*SC* 55, 53).

❖ More active and thoughtful participation through the use of the vernacular, expressed in a shift among the laity away from private devotions during the Mass, to a sense of the celebration of salvation by the parish community (*SC* 54).

❖ The greater stress on the role of Scripture and proclamation in liturgy, expressed through the clear structure in the Mass of the Liturgy of the Word and the Liturgy of the Eucharist (*SC* 51-52, 56).

❖ More devout and active participation of the faithful, assisted by the recovery of the simple and intelligible structure of the early liturgies of the Church, through the removal of later duplications and complexities and the restoration of elements that had been lost (*SC* 50).

❖ Primacy given to the celebration of Sunday, as the weekly Easter, rather than the commemoration of saints.

7.2   Shadows Cast Over the Reform of the Liturgy

While acknowledging the success of the liturgical reforms inaugurated by the Council, particularly in forming 'a more conscious, active and fruitful participation in the Holy Sacrifice of the Altar on the part of the faithful', Pope John Paul II also recognised that 'shadows are not lacking' in its implementation. (Pope John Paul II, Apostolic Letter, *Vicesimus quintus annus*, 12-13):

> In this regard it is not possible to be silent about the abuses, even quite grave ones, against the nature of the Liturgy and the Sacraments as well as the tradition and the authority of the Church, which in our day not infrequently plague liturgical celebrations... In some places the perpetration of liturgical abuses has become almost habitual, a fact which obviously cannot be allowed and must cease. Congregation for Divine Worship and Discipline of the Sacraments, *Redemptionis Sacramentum*, 4).

There are a number of shadows cast over the genuine reform of the liturgy that diminish us all, because they often sow the seeds of disunity and discord:

7.2.1   The Shadow of False Freedom

I think there has been an undue fondness for liturgical innovation in certain quarters, with some thinking they are free to do what they think best in the liturgy, irrespective of what is laid down in the rubrics or the principles of the *General Instruction of the Roman Missal*.

Aidan Nichols has observed that *Sacrosanctum Concilium* did not give everyone *carte blanche* for endless innovations to the liturgy according to the personal tastes of the parish or group within the parish. As Catholics we do not have an illusory liberty by which we think we may do what we wish, but we do have the liberty to do what is fitting and right. This is true of divine laws from God and for ecclesiastical laws.

7.2.2 The Light of Obedience

In order to counter the influence of this false concept of freedom, it is not unreasonable to hope that every priest, deacon and parish community will, without exception, follow the *General Instruction of the Roman Missal*, the rubrics of the Roman Missal, and the Congregation for Divine Worship's, *Redemptionis Sacramentum*.

I am certain that it is only through observing the norms published by the authority of the Church, that the genuine reform of the sacred liturgy will be finally achieved in our diocese. 'Christ's faithful have a right to worship according to the provisions of their own rite approved by the lawful pastors of the Church'. (*Canon* 214).

> The observance of the norms published by the authority of the Church requires conformity of thought and of word, of external action and of the application of the heart. A merely external observation of norms would obviously be contrary to the nature of the Sacred Liturgy, in which Christ himself wishes to gather his Church, so that together with Himself she will be "one body and one spirit". Congregation for Divine Worship and Discipline of the Sacraments, *Redemptionis Sacramentum*, 5).

7.2.3 The Shadow of Ignorance

There is an ancient principle of the Church that recognises the intimate connection between liturgy and doctrine, *Lex Orandi, Lex Credendi* [The law of prayer is the law of belief]. If we get doctrine wrong, we get liturgy wrong, and if we get liturgy wrong, we get doctrine wrong.

Over the years I have noticed an over-emphasis on the humanity of Jesus, as if his major characteristic was as a Jewish prophet, or moral teacher or political figure, ignoring or down-playing His incarnation as the Son of God, the second person of the Holy Trinity. Yes, he was a Jewish prophet, and a moral teacher, and a political figure, but He was also so much more than this! As St Thomas the Apostle proclaimed, 'My Lord and my God!' (*Jn* 20:28).

This one dimensional, humanistic portrayal of Jesus without the incarnational reality, often results in a moralising, shallow liturgy that over-emphasises the horizontal that is the human community. Liturgy is not primarily about creating the experience of community, it should be about adoration of God. (Aidan Nichols, *Beyond the Blue Glass*, vol. 1, p.143-144).

7.2.4 The Light of Doctrine

I am firmly convinced that clergy and people in the Church need to re-discover the truth of the Church's doctrinal portrayal of Jesus Christ if we are to attain the authentic renewal of the liturgy. It is only through the Church's holistic doctrine of Christ, founded on Scripture, that enables us to see Jesus is truly God and truly man. Therefore I recommend the following as sources for the authentic Catholic understanding of Jesus Christ:

- ✓ *The Catechism of the Catholic Church*. Section Two. Chapter two. *I believe in Jesus Christ, the Only Son of God*. (CCC 430-682).

- ✓ Pope Benedict, *Jesus of Nazareth*, Bloomsbury, 2007.

- ✓ Cardinal Walter Kasper, *The God of Jesus Christ*, SCM, 1983. & *Jesus the Christ*, Burns and Oates, 1977.

- ✓ Fr John Redford, *Bad, Mad or God? Proving the Divinity of Christ from St John's Gospel*, St Pauls, 2004, & *Born of a Virgin: Proving the Miracle from the Gospels*, St Pauls, 2007.

7.2.5 The Shadow of Consumerism

The other day I heard a pastiche of Descartes' famous philosophical aphorism, 'I think, therefore I am', which has now become, 'I shop, therefore I am'. I think this playful joke points to a deeper, more troubling reality - the extent to which our outlook on life and basic relationships have become unconsciously conditioned by the illusory power of consumer capitalism.

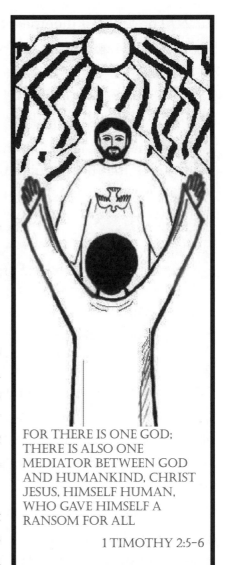

FOR THERE IS ONE GOD; THERE IS ALSO ONE MEDIATOR BETWEEN GOD AND HUMANKIND, CHRIST JESUS, HIMSELF HUMAN, WHO GAVE HIMSELF A RANSOM FOR ALL

1 TIMOTHY 2:5-6

Where this hedonistic, consumerist mentality is present it reduces the liturgy to a form of entertainment. This shifts the priority of worship away from the adoration of God, to revolve around the personal likes and dislikes of the clergy and congregation.

I am sure many of you are familiar with the symptoms of this dysfunction in the life of the Church:

- The priest reduced to being almost an entertainer whose desire is to keep the interest of his community;

- Members of the congregation who need constant novelty and stimulation;

- Laity who 'shop around' from one parish to the next until they find the 'service' that meets their particular tastes in liturgy.

All of these symptoms are manifestations of a deeper malady, which is a lack of true faith. Such shallow faith trivialises the liturgy to the proportions of man's whims and caprices.

7.2.6 The Light of True Faith

To counter this false spirituality of consumerism, I propose that we need to recover a sense of true faith in the living God. If people have true faith they will not have a subjective focus on themselves and their transient needs, but will instead have an objective focus on God.

Anscar Vonier, Abbot of Buckfast Abbey, wrote in his famous work on the sacrifice of the Mass, *A Key to the Doctrine of the Eucharist*, that before thinking about how we benefit as individuals through participation at Mass, we need to become aware of a greater reality expressed through the Mass:

> Before it is at all possible to think about man's enrichment through the grace of Christ's redemption we have to assume that much greater result of Christ's sacrifice on the Cross which is aptly expressed in the term "Atonement", by which is meant, not directly the benefit of man, but the benefit of God: that full restoration of what had been taken from God through man's sin, His honour and glory. Christ's act on the Cross has given back to the Father all that was ever taken away from Him by man, and the divine rights have been fully restored. (Abbot Vonier, *A Key to the Doctrine of the Eucharist*, p. 2)

First and foremost, the sacrifice of the Mass is for the benefit of God, not because anything we do can benefit God but because through the Mass we participate in Jesus' sacrifice on the Cross. It is God who benefits God. As *Sacrosanctum Concilium* 5 states, 'Thus in Christ "there came forth the perfect satisfaction needed for our reconciliation, and we received the means for giving worthy worship to God"'.

In the sacrament of the Eucharist, the very death, resurrection and glorification of Christ are re-presented for us in a way that allows us to enter the mystery of salvation. It is for this reason that the sacrament is said to 're-present' the paschal mystery. It is the faith of the Church that every time the Eucharist is celebrated and the priest consecrates the bread and wine making them the body and blood of Christ, the holy sacrifice of Christ's death on the cross and his resurrection to new life are re-presented for us - sacramentally but truly in a way that we participate now in this sacred action.

The Church never ceases to present to the Father Christ's 'sacrifice of praise': "You know how firmly we believe in you and dedicate ourselves to you. We offer you this sacrifice of praise for ourselves and those who are dear to us". (*Eucharistic Prayer One*).

It should be apparent to everyone participating in the Mass that the focus must be on God, not upon ourselves or on our efforts. Only one thing is required for our participation - it's not our interest, or our satisfaction, or our happiness but our single-minded faith that is necessary. Interest, satisfaction and happiness will follow as secondary effects of our self-forgetfulness in worship.

Sacrosanctum Concilium 11 - 12 recommends a number of actions by the faithful that promote participation with true faith in the liturgy:

✓ In order that the liturgy may be able to produce its full effects it is necessary that we prepare beforehand, through reading and praying with the Scripture readings and the prayers of the Mass. In this way our minds will be attuned with our voices and we will be disposed to co-operate with 'heavenly grace'.

✓ I recommend the CTS *Simple Prayer book* which contains a section of prayers for before and after receiving Holy Communion that can help one focus on God. It is a good idea to distribute copies among the pews, so people can have easy access to them for personal devotions.

✓ I recommend that parishes to establish Sunday Preparation Groups, to enable clergy and people to study and pray the readings and / or prayers of the forthcoming Sunday Mass. The forthcoming *Wednesday Word* initiative will be very helpful for our primary school families to share the Sunday Scriptures together.

7.3   Prayer Makes Liturgy Real in our Lives.

We need to enable the power and presence of the liturgy to sweep beyond our sanctuaries and churches into our homes, schools, colleges and workplaces. As Archbishop Oscar Romero puts it:

> When we leave Mass, we ought to go out the way Moses descended Mount Sinai: with his face shining, with his heart brave and strong to face the world's difficulties. (Archbishop Oscar Romero).

Why did Moses' face shine when he came down from Mount Sinai? Reflecting on this mystery, I think Moses' face shone because he had been in the presence of God talking with Him as a friend. In other words, Moses was transformed through personal prayer, through his personal relationship with God.

Many people recognise that one of the most beautiful and powerful sections of the *Catechism of the Catholic Church* is the fourth pillar, on Christian Prayer. A major contributor to this was Fr Jean Corbon OP, a Greek Catholic from Beirut, who often worked on the section on prayer in his basement during shelling occurring during the destructive civil war. In a wonderful book on liturgy he wrote, 'It is through the prayer of the heart that liturgy becomes life'. (Jean Corbon, *The Wellspring of Worship*, p. 206). The praying heart is the personal sanctuary where we meet the living God. As *Gaudium et Spes* puts it:

> For by his interior qualities he outstrips the whole sum of mere things. He attains to these inward depths whenever he enters his own heart. God, who probes the heart, awaits him there. (*Gaudium et Spes*, 14).

If we want a renewal of the sacredness and glory of liturgy, we must start with renewing a sense of the sacred in our own hearts through faithful, persistent prayer. As Fr Jean Corbon so beautifully expresses it, we must make an altar of our heart. Through prayer, the presence of the Lord is in 'the heart as on an altar on which the Holy Spirit places and engraves the eternal Gospel: Jesus.' (Jean Corbon, *The Wellspring of Worship*, p. 210-211). Through the celebration of the Mass, Jesus invites us into His prayer to the Father through the power and presence of the Holy Spirit in our hearts and our community.

Scripture must be at the heart of our prayer as individuals and communities, because the Word of God will teach us how to pray:

> We ourselves are brought into conversation with God by the word of God. The God who speaks in the Bible teaches us how to speak with him ourselves. Particularly in the book of Psalms, he gives us the words with which we can address him, with which we can bring our life, with all its highpoints and lowpoints, into conversation with him, so that life itself thereby becomes a movement towards him. (Pope Benedict XVI, *Address to representatives from the world of culture*, France, September 2008).

7.4   Sacred Liturgy - Objectives for the Renewal of the Church

7.4.1   Cherishing Continuity

Sacrosanctum Concilium envisaged the renewal of the liturgy as entailing careful changes that facilitated the active participation of the laity balanced with preserving what is essential to the tradition of the Church:

> In order that sound tradition be retained, and yet the way remain open to legitimate progress, a careful investigation - theological, historical and pastoral - should always be made into each part of the liturgy which is to be revised... Finally, there must be no innovations unless the good of the Church genuinely and certainly requires them, and care must be taken that any new forms adopted should in some way grow organically from forms already existing. (*SC* 23)

After a sustained period of change, it is time that we cherished the continuity of our liturgy with the living tradition of the Church. No one would want to set back the great success of the Council in fostering - through the use of the vernacular - the active participation of all the faithful in the celebration of the Mass. This must be protected and further encouraged through the more faithful translation that is in preparation.

However, much that the Council wanted to preserve has, until recently, been in danger of being forgotten. It is time that we remembered that we are part of the Latin-rite Catholic Church. This is our heritage, this is our culture.

The Council Fathers never envisaged a totally vernacular liturgy, but quite specifically decided that the Mass should contain both Latin and the vernacular. This is what *Sacrosanctum Concilium* actually lays down about the use of the vernacular:

> (1) The use of the Latin language, with due respect to particular law, is to be preserved in the Latin rites. (2) But since the use of the vernacular, whether in the Mass, the administration of the sacraments, or in other parts of the liturgy, may frequently be of great advantage to the people, a wider use may be made of it, especially in readings, directives and in some prayers and chants. (*SC* 36).

I recommend the following actions to cherish continuity in the liturgy:

✓ When we apply the principle set out in *Sacrosanctum Concilium* 23 that 'sound tradition' must be retained, it makes obvious sense that Latin should still play a regular part in celebration of the Mass, such as the *Gloria*, the *Credo*, *Sanctus*, *Pater noster* and *Agnus Dei*.

✓ I recommend that everyone should familiarise themselves with the Latin common prayers. The CTS *Simple Prayer book* contains the Mass in English and Latin.

✓ Also following the principle of retaining 'sound tradition', I propose that efforts are made to recover those beautiful and moving services that have been lost, such as *Tenebrae* on Maundy Thursday. I understand that some parishes in the diocese of Lancaster are already striving to recover these treasures of our heritage.

"LOOK, THE VIRGIN SHALL CONCEIVE AND BEAR A SON, AND THEY SHALL NAME HIM EMMANUEL,: WHICH MEANS "GOD IS WITH US."

MATTHEW 1:23

✓ I would encourage parishes , where possible, to pray the Office of the Church together - morning and evening prayer.

✓ To those 'stable groups of faithful' availing themselves of the extraordinary form I would make the following suggestions as a pastor in the Church in accordance with the Motu Proprio *Summorum Pontificum*:

❍ Active participation in the life of your parish is essential to being in full communion with the Catholic Church. Therefore, it is my earnest hope that you will not abandon participation in your parish's use of the ordinary form.

❍ Avoid habitual travelling around to participate in the extraordinary form if this means you are no longer an active member of your local parish.

❍ Any attitude of superiority due to participation in the extraordinary form is to be avoided as a danger to the unity and well-being of the Church.

❍ Equally, there must be no lack of charity or hospitality towards those 'stable groups of faithful' who 'continue to adhere with great love and affection to the earlier liturgical forms' as this too damages the unity and well-being of our local Church in communion with the See of Rome.

To conclude, let me be clear, I consider that the use of Latin with the vernacular is not about the rejection of the Second Vatican Council, but is about being true to what the Council Fathers actually discerned as necessary for Latin-rite Catholics.

7.4.2 Regaining the Sense of Glory

In the earthly liturgy we take part in a foretaste of that heavenly liturgy which is celebrated in the Holy City of Jerusalem toward which we journey as pilgrims, where Christ is sitting at the right hand of God, Minister of the holies and of the true tabernacle. With all the warriors of the heavenly army we sing a hymn of glory to the Lord; venerating the memory of the saints, we hope for some part and fellowship with them; we eagerly await the Saviour, Our Lord Jesus Christ, until he our life shall appear and we too will appear with him in glory. (*SC* 8).

The Extraordinary Synod on the Second Vatican Council (1985) recommended that the implementation of the Council particularly required at the present time, that 'the liturgy must favour the sense of the sacred and make it shine forth. It must be permeated by the spirit of reverence, adoration and glory of God.' (Extraordinary Synod of Bishops, *The Final Report*).

The challenge at the heart of authentic Catholic liturgy is to realise and reflect the balance between the divine and human reality Christ instituted as His Church. In practise this means being sensitive to the balance between the visible and invisible, the temporal and the eternal, community and the sacred. (Aidan Nichols). An imbalance between any of these elements results in distortions to the liturgy.

Over the years I have observed in some of our parishes an over-emphasis on the community dimension of Mass that has at times eclipsed reverence and adoration of the divine. Of course, the role of the community is essential, but at times there are diversions and distractions, such as:

- Performances within the Mass;
- Concert pieces;
- Extended signs of peace;
- Endless commentaries and
- Prayers of the Faithful that become collects or mini-homilies.

Such distortions can reflect the common Christological error of emphasising the humanity of Jesus, to the exclusions of any meaningful sense of His divinity.

I am certain that for liturgy to enable us to participate in the life of the Holy Trinity we must maintain a sensitive balance between human participation and reverence of the divine.

Towards this goal, we must constantly strive for beauty and reverence in our liturgy. As Pope Benedict XVI expressed it in Notre-Dame Cathedral, Paris:

Certainly, the beauty of our celebrations can never be sufficiently cultivated, fostered and refined, for nothing can be too beautiful for God, who is himself infinite Beauty. Yet our earthly liturgies will never be more than a pale reflection of the liturgy celebrated in the Jerusalem on high, the goal of our pilgrimage on earth. May our own celebrations nonetheless resemble that liturgy as closely as possible and grant us a foretaste of it! (Pope Benedict XVI, *Homily at Notre-Dame Cathedral*, France, September 2008).

I recommend the following actions to foster the correct balance required for authentic liturgy:

✓ That parishes establish - following proper formation - a liturgy committee. (A Sacramental Priority of the *Final Proposals* of the *Fit for Mission? Parish* review).

✓ Cultivate the recognition that the Parish church is primarily the house of God, rather than a community centre. The Church is more than the assembly of like-minded and well-motivated people. It is a divine and human reality instituted by Christ to lead us to God. 'Christ is always present in his Church, especially in her liturgical celebrations' (*SC* 7).

✓ Silence fosters an atmosphere of prayer and adoration. I don't recommend absolute silence, as charity must be the predominant value expressed through neighbourliness and friendship. However, there must not be conversations or texting immediately before, during or just after the liturgy. Mobile phones must be switched off in church.

✓ Parish churches should be known as places where sacred music, art and vestments are treasured and used to assist the celebration of liturgy and devotions. Parishes should be known as centres of excellence in the celebration of the liturgy, for processions, vigils and devotions. Steps should be taken to protect and conserve old vestments and sacred vessels.

✓ *The Rite of Christian Initiation of Adults and Children* must be presented first and foremost as an initiation into the life of Christ, and not merely as an initiation into community membership.

✓ Due to the materialistic focus of contemporary men and women, we have a vital entry point to teach the value and significance of sacraments. Through the sacraments God shows us He cherishes the material, such as bread and wine, water and oil. Therefore, I recommend that clergy introduce a regular series of homilies, based on the *Lectionary* and the *Catechism of the Catholic Church*, that teach Catholic sacramental theology, such as the role of signs and symbols, and the value and significance of the seven sacraments.

✓ Parish preparation of children for First Holy Communion must thoroughly prepare them for this sacrament, emphasizing and teaching the Real Presence. As I wrote in *Fit for Mission? Schools* we are faced with an urgent crisis regarding belief in this sublime doctrine.

✓ I am also sure that the witness of prayerful and beautiful Eucharistic adoration will convey the power of our belief in the Real Presence of the Lord.

✓ I encourage the use of the sacrament of the sick for those in need.

7.4.3   Regaining a Sense of Sin and Redemption

Cardinal Joseph Ratzinger observed that in the post-conciliar period the term 'the divine sacrifice of the Eucharist' has fallen into disuse, being replaced by the term 'supper'. Central concepts of the redemption such as sacrifice, expiation, supplication and reparatory satisfaction are very difficult for our contemporaries to grasp:

> Contemporary thought can no longer imagine that human fault can wound God, and still less that it would require an expiation equal to that which constitutes the cross of Christ. The same holds true for vicarious substitution: we can scarcely imagine anything like that; our image of man has become too individualistic for that. That is why the crisis of the liturgy is rooted in central notions about man. (Joseph Ratzinger, *Theology of the Liturgy in 'Oriens'*, *www.oriensjournal*).

I strongly believe that this loss of understanding of sacrifice, reparation and atonement is tied to the equally striking loss of a sense of sin that we are witnessing in our society. There is a definite link between awareness of sin and guilt and an understanding of the need for sacrifice and reparation to make things good. Sacrifice is the expression of Christ's love for us sinners, whose wounds are healed by His blood.

Pope John Paul II identified a loss of a sense of sin as a major problem within the Church and society in general, which he saw as an expression of a wider denial of God.

One of the influences behind the disappearance of the sense of sin can be traced to a catechetical approach that wrongly identifies a sense of sin with a morbid feeling of guilt or with the mere transgression of legal norms or cultural conditions (Pope John Paul II, Post synod exhortation, *Reconciliatio et Paenitentia*, 18).

This erroneous catechetical approach has its origins in the *uncritical* adoption of psychological and sociological models, such as the so called 'person-centred theory' of counselling with its criticism of moral judgement as 'judgementalism'.

We must never forget our capacity for self-deception as well as our readiness to reduce conscience to an 'excuse mechanism' (Ratzinger). As it is expressed in Psalm 19: 12, *'Who can detect his own failings? Wash out my hidden faults.'*

The absence of any sense of guilt could be a sign of profound spiritual desolation. Guilt is to spiritual health what pain is to physical health: a warning that something is wrong and so needs to be healed (Robert Spaemann). God's mercy makes no sense without it.

In my life-time, we have gone from an exaggerated sense of sin, which focused too heavily on punishment, to a lack of a sense of sin, which focuses too heavily on undemanding forgiveness. As Pope John Paul II puts it:

> From seeing sin everywhere they pass to not recognizing it anywhere; from too much emphasis on the fear of eternal punishment they pass to preaching a love of God that excludes any punishment deserved by sin; from severity in trying to correct erroneous consciences they pass to a kind of respect for conscience which excludes the duty of telling the truth. (Pope John Paul II, Post Synodal Exhortation, *Reconciliatio et Paenitentia*, 18)

✓ I recommend that clergy use their homilies - particularly during the penitential seasons of Advent and Lent - to present reflection and exhortation about the seriousness and consequences of sin, and the wonderful gift of the redemption.

✓ It is an urgent priority that our parishes promote the healing power of the Sacrament of Reconciliation.

✓ I also recommend a devotion to the Stations of the Cross and the shroud of Turin which present a striking visible witness to the redemptive sufferings of Christ. As Pope Benedict XVI wrote in his meditation on the Stations of the Cross, 'Jesus is nailed to the Cross. The shroud of Turin gives us an idea of the unbelievable cruelty of this procedure...Let us halt before this image of pain, before the suffering Son of God. Let us look upon Him at times of presumptuousness and pleasure, in order to learn to respect limits and to see the superficiality of all merely material goods. (Pope Benedict XVI, *Way of the Cross*, p. 47).

Key One: The Constitution on Sacred Liturgy	
Areas for reflection	**Suggested Actions**

• How do I ensure that the observance of norms in Sacred Liturgy penetrates my heart so I experience through this my unity in Christ's Church, 'one body and one spirit'?
 	
• Do I keep my 'focus' on God during the Mass?
 	
• Do I attain self-forgetfulness in worship? What helps and hinders me in this?
 	
• How do I ensure that the observance of norms in Sacred Liturgy penetrates my heart so I experience through this my unity in Christ's Church, 'one body and one spirit'?
 	
• Do I keep my 'focus' on God during the Mass?
 	
• Do I attain self-forgetfulness in worship? What helps and hinders me in this?
	• Ensure your parish is following the *General Instruction of the Roman Missal*, the rubrics of the Roman Missal, and the Congregation for Divine Worship's, *Redemptionis Sacramentum*
	
	• Read and reflect on the following:
	
	  • The *Catechism of the Catholic Church*. Section Two. Chapter two. I believe in Jesus Christ, the Only Son of God. (CCC 430-682).
	
	  • Pope Benedict, *Jesus of Nazareth*, Bloomsbury, 2007.
	
	  • Cardinal Walter Kasper, *The God of Jesus Christ*, SCM, 1983 & *Jesus the Christ*, Burns and Oates, 1977.
	
	  • Fr John Redford, *Bad, Mad or God? Proving the Divinity of Christ from St John's Gospel*, St Pauls, 2004, & *Born of a Virgin: Proving the Miracle from the Gospels*, St Pauls, 2007.

Key One: The Constitution on Sacred Liturgy *(continued)*	
Areas for reflection	**Suggested Actions**
• What do I understand when Christ's sacrifice is described as "that full restoration of what has been taken from God through man's sin, His honour and glory"? • How do I ensure a balance between the visible and invisible, the temporal and the eternal, community and the sacred? • How do I deepen my understanding of the Real Presence? Can I explain my belief to others?	• Ensure you set aside adequate time to prepare before Mass. If not already established, set up a 'Sunday Preparation Group'. • Use the CTS Simple prayer book - or equivalent - for prayers before and after receiving Holy Communion. • Make the common prayers in Latin a regular part of your celebration of Mass. • Participate in your parish, where possible, in the Office of the Church, morning and evening prayers and in traditional services such as *Tenebrae* on Maundy Thursday night. • Ensure you cultivate the recognition of the Parish Church as primarily the house of God by avoiding conversations immediately before, during or just after the liturgy inside the Church. Ensure mobiles are switched off and do not text in Church. • Protect and conserve vestments and sacred vessels. • Introduce a regular series of homilies, based on the lectionary and the *CCC*, that teach Catholic sacramental theology, such as the role of signs and symbols and the value and significance of the seven sacraments. Ensure, particularly during Lent and Advent, that homilies present reflection and exhortation on the seriousness and consequences of sin and the wonderful gift of the redemption. • Make a regular commitment to Eucharistic adoration. • Promote and utilise the healing power of the Sacrament of Reconciliation. • Complete devotion to the Stations of the Cross. Use meditation on the shroud of Turin to assist understanding of Christ's sacrifice.

8   Key Two: The Dogmatic Constitution on Divine Revelation

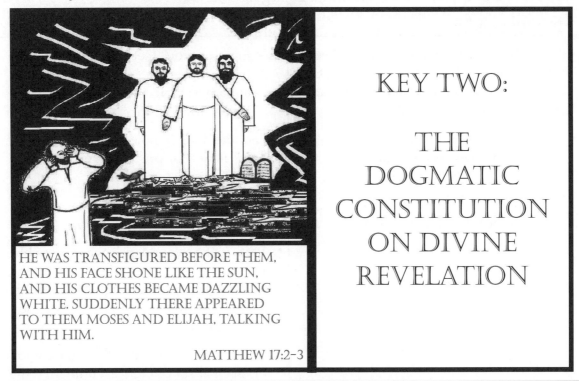

HE WAS TRANSFIGURED BEFORE THEM, AND HIS FACE SHONE LIKE THE SUN, AND HIS CLOTHES BECAME DAZZLING WHITE. SUDDENLY THERE APPEARED TO THEM MOSES AND ELIJAH, TALKING WITH HIM.

MATTHEW 17:2-3

KEY TWO:

THE DOGMATIC CONSTITUTION ON DIVINE REVELATION

Divine Revelation: The Word of God, proclaimed in liturgy, gathers the Church together and calls for our response of love.

Each day at the opening of proceedings during the Second Vatican Council, a deacon led the liturgical enthroning of the Gospel. Speaking to the priests and permanent deacons of Rome in Lent 2008 Pope Benedict XVI explained its profound significance for truly understanding the Council:

'This liturgical enthroning of the Word of God each day during the Council was always for us a gesture of great importance: It told us who was the true Lord of that assembly; it told us that the Word of God was on the throne and that we exercise our ministry to listen and to interpret, to offer to the others this word. It is broadly significant for all that we do: enthroning in the world the Word of God, the living word, Christ. May it really be Him who governs our personal life and our life in the parishes...'(*Pope Benedict XVI's address to the Roman Clergy*, 11th February 2008).

I see this simple liturgical act of daily enthroning the Word of God during the Ecumenical Council, before the shrine of St Peter, in the presence of the Pope and bishops of the world, beautifully crystallising the Catholic understanding of the vital and inseparable relationship between Scripture, Tradition and the Magisterium in the life of the Church and individual Catholics:

It is clear, therefore, that sacred Tradition, sacred Scripture and the teaching authority of the Church, in accord with God's most wise design, are so linked and joined together that one cannot stand without the others, and that all together and each in its own way under the action of the one Holy Spirit contribute effectively to the salvation of souls. (*DV* 10).

8.1 Keeping the Bible Alive!

Despite questions over its post conciliar reception, and the extent that it has really been taken to heart, *Dei Verbum* has been credited with the renaissance of active engagement with the Word of God among the faithful. Its achievements include:

❖ Clergy and people better educated in knowledge and spirituality of the Bible, due to moving away from only having contact with scripture through the catechism or missal, to direct and personal contact with the Old Testament and New Testament. (*DV* 22).

❖ The biblical renewal of liturgy, theology and catechesis, through re-evaluating the importance of the Bible as the book of the Church. (*DV* 21).

❖ A flourishing of Catholic biblical studies, based on a balanced use of the historical critical method. (*DV* 12).

❖ The publication and distribution of Catholic editions of the Bible, with study notes and references, such as the New Jerusalem Bible, and the *CTS New Catholic Bible*.

❖ The increasing use of the Bible in prayer, such as the growing popularity of *Lectio Divina* and *Ignatian imaginative prayer*. Pope Benedict XVI is convinced that if *Dei Verbum's* advocacy of the diligent reading of Sacred Scripture accompanied by prayer (*DV* 25) is embraced more fully by the faithful, 'it will bring to the Church a new spiritual springtime'. (*Address of His Holiness Benedict XVI to the participants in the International Congress Organised to Commemorate the 40th Anniversary of the Dogmatic Constitution on Divine Revelation*, 2005).

❖ Fostering a deeper ecumenical co-operation and agreement based on a common love, reverence and study of scripture. As Archbishop John Onaiyekan, Nigeria, said in his speech to the International Congress on *Dei Verbum*, the move towards a common understanding of Scripture has brought about 'a great revolution in the relationship between our different churches'. (John Onaiyekan, *From Dei Verbum to Novo Millenio Ineunte*).

8.2 Taking Risks for the Word of God

Reading *Dei Verbum* again I am conscious of the fact that the Council Fathers were very much aware of the risks they were taking in promoting, say, the use of the historical critical method, or the wider distribution of the Bible among the laity.

Some of you may be surprised that I'm writing about these decisions of the Council being risks, but this is to underestimate the very real dangers of misusing the Bible in research or personal use to the life of the Church and the well being of the individual.

What is a risk? *The Oxford English Dictionary* defines it as a *hazard or chance of bad consequences, exposure to chance of injury or loss'*.

But life is about weighing up risks and taking sensible precautions that mitigate the dangers of injury or loss. On the whole, the advantages of furthering research on Scripture and encouraging the wider use of the Bible have outweighed the dangers to the Church.

However, I consider it a good idea at this time for us all to reacquaint ourselves with the risks, and avail ourselves of the precautions against harm advocated by the Second Vatican Council.

8.3   The Risk of Misusing the Bible.

> The Church has always venerated the divine Scriptures just as she venerates the body of the Lord, since, especially in the sacred liturgy, she unceasingly receives and offers to the faithful the bread of life from the table both of God's word and of Christ's body. She has always maintained them, and continues to do so, together with sacred tradition, as the supreme rule of faith, since, as inspired by God and committed once and for all to writing, they impart the Word of God Himself without change, and make the voice of the Holy Spirit resound in the words of the prophets and Apostles. (*DV* 21).

A while ago I attended a diocesan meeting at which I was surprised to hear a Catholic stand up and object to the distribution of a church document because she stridently argued that all we needed was the Bible!

It amazes me that 40 years after the promulgation of *Dei Verbum's* carefully nuanced presentation of the inextricable relationship between Scripture and Tradition that I can hear a Catholic protest the equivalent of, "*Sola Scriptura*! Only the Bible and nothing but the Bible!"

This misunderstanding of the role of Scripture in the Church is not an isolated one. Many mistakenly believe that for an action or belief of the Catholic Church to be valid or acceptable, it has to find an explicit, literal mandate in the written word of Scripture. A version of biblical fundamentalism has developed among sections of the Catholic Church, with some Catholics demanding, "Where is it in the Bible?" If they can't personally find it in the Bible, they hold they don't have to believe it! Such a mistaken attitude can be found among theologians, catechists, journalists on Catholic periodicals and ordinary parishioners.

I agree with Cardinal Avery Dulles when he observes that some Catholics mistakenly believe that the Second Vatican Council 'gave priority to Scripture as the written word of God, and demoted tradition to the status of a secondary norm, to be tested against the higher norm of Scripture'. (Avery Dulles, *Vatican II: The Myth and the Reality*).

8.4   The True Use of Scripture

> Through our gospel He called you to this so that you should claim as your own the glory of our Lord Jesus Christ. Stand firm, then, brothers, and keep the traditions that we taught you, whether by word of mouth or by letter. (2 *Th* 2:13-15).

The Council clearly presents the Catholic understanding of the place and role of Scripture in the life of the Church and individual.

Dei Verbum starts from the premise that revelation is founded not only on the word Christ preached but also in the whole living experience of His person: 'the Apostles, who by their oral preaching, by example and by observances handed on what they had received from the lips of Christ, from living with Him and from what He did, or what they had learned through the promptings of the Holy Spirit '(*DV* 7). We can conclude from this that the Word of God includes and also transcends the written word of Scripture.

The Council places Scripture within the framework of Tradition, with the objective content of Tradition - the teaching of the Church, the life of the Church and the worship of the Church - including and surpassing that of Scripture. *Dei Verbum* 8 states that Scripture is the inspired and privileged expression of the pre-existing apostolic Tradition, and is not an independent or separate norm. Therefore, the Tradition of the Church takes a logical precedence over Scripture.

As Karl Rahner puts it, it was a historical necessity that the apostolic preaching took concrete form as Scripture, but by 'becoming a book it does not become an independent herald and norm of the faith'. Post-biblical Tradition is also necessary to transmit, interpret and explain the preaching expressed as Scripture. (Karl Rahner, *Encyclopaedia of Theology*, p.1550).

> And so the apostolic preaching, which is expressed in a special way in the inspired books, was to be preserved by a continuous succession of preachers until the end of time. Therefore the apostles, handing on what they themselves had received, warn the faithful to hold fast to the traditions which they learned either by word of mouth or by letter (cf. 2 *Th* 2:15), and to fight in defence of the faith handed on once and for all (cf, *Jud* 3). (*DV* 8).

So, we may ask, what is the role of Scripture in the life of the Church and the individual? *Dei Verbum* makes clear the primacy of Scripture in the life of the Church, which is 'nourished and regulated by Sacred Scripture' (*DV* 12). While both Tradition and Scripture together are the norm for the faith of the Church, it has been 'expressed in a special way in the inspired books' (*DV* 8), so that Tradition must always be related back to Scripture and measured by it through the guidance and teaching of the Church.

As *Dei Verbum* makes clear, the Magisterium is the sole authentic interpreter of the word of God, in Scripture and Tradition, not the individual with their own copy of the Bible (*DV* 10).

I propose the following for consideration and action by the diocese and our parishes:

- ✓ Encourage all the faithful to read the Bible, 'For in the sacred books, the Father who is in heaven meets His children with great love and speaks with them; and the force and power in the word of God is so great that it remains the support and energy of the Church, the strength of faith for her sons, the food of the soul, the pure and perennial source of spiritual life'. (*DV* 21).

✓ Promote Catholic translations of the Bible, such as *The New Jerusalem Bible, Study Edition*, and the *Catholic edition of the Revised Standard Version*.

✓ One of my roles is - according to *Dei Verbum* - to give the faithful entrusted to me 'suitable instruction in the right use of the divine books, especially the New Testament and above all the Gospels'. (*DV* 25). Therefore, I propose to explore ways to further fulfil my responsibility to promote the Catholic use of Scripture in my diocese.

8.5   The Risk of Growing Dissent

Since *Dei Verbum's* consolidation of Pope Pius XII's groundbreaking encyclical *Divino Afflante Spiritu*, which opened Catholic biblical studies to modern research methods, it is generally recognised that 'biblical studies have made great progress in the Catholic Church'. (The Pontifical Biblical Commission, *The Interpretation of the Bible in the Church*, p. 30). In particular the historical-critical method, which seeks to understand the text in its historical context, is indispensible in a proper interpretation of the bible.

As Pope Benedict XVI recently wrote in his superlative work, *Jesus of Nazareth: From the Baptism in the Jordan to the Transfiguration*, 'it is of the very essence of biblical faith to be about real historical events' (p. xv).

> Since God speaks in sacred Scripture through men in human fashion, the interpreter of sacred Scripture, in order to see clearly what God wanted to communicate to us, should carefully investigate what meaning the sacred writers really intended, and what God wanted to manifest by means of their words. (*DV* 12).

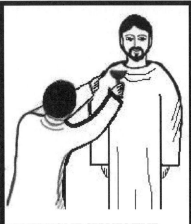

"EVERYONE SERVES THE GOOD WINE FIRST, AND THEN THE INFERIOR WINE AFTER THE GUESTS HAVE BECOME DRUNK. BUT YOU HAVE KEPT THE GOOD WINE UNTIL NOW."

JOHN 2:10

However, the acceptance of the validity of modern research methods by the Church has not been without risks of misuse by some theologians, which has cast shadows across the lives of the faithful through - among other things - irresponsible and inauthentic catechesis.

As a consequence, among certain circles, Catholics have assumed an extreme scepticism regarding Scripture and the content of faith. This scepticism rejects the action of God in the world through miracles. The Pontifical Biblical Commission has captured the opinions of this rationalist counter-faith very well as follows:

■ There is no supernatural order.

■ God does not intervene in the world in strict revelation.

■ Miracles are not possible and do not exist.

■ Faith is incompatible with historical 'truth'.

- *A priori* there is no historical value in the documents of revelation.

- Apostolic testimony is suspect and reflects the creativity of the community in the early Church'.

(Pontifical Biblical Commission, *An Instruction on the Historical Truth of the Gospels*).

These mistaken views are often the source of persistent dissent by some in the Church and are disseminated by certain Catholic journals at home and abroad. It is sad to say that there are Catholics, sometimes in positions of authority in education and catechesis, who hold some or all of these opinions deriving from the misuse of the historical-critical method.

Let me be clear, disagreement and debate between people of good-will about *reformable* ideas and practises are to be encouraged in the Church. However, when such disagreement and debate becomes public dissent through organised opposition, lobbying and campaigns, there is a danger to the unity and well being of the Church. (Avery Dulles).

I've also observed that Catholics who privately dissent from certain doctrines and disciplines of the Church are often prey to growing anger and disillusionment with the Church in general. What starts out as a doubt or scepticism due to some piece of historical-critical research, taken in isolation, becomes a type of creeping doubt about the certainty of doctrine. Doubting the historical authenticity of a saying or deed of Christ in the Gospel, they can eventually come to doubt the truth of the Church.

THIS IS THE DISCIPLE WHO IS TESTIFYING TO THESE THINGS AND HAS WRITTEN THEM, AND WE KNOW THAT HIS TESTIMONY IS TRUE

JOHN 21:24

Such doubts can lead to discontent with the Church, often focused against the person of the reigning Pope and the local bishop. It is common for bishops to receive letters and emails angrily demanding the Church change a doctrine of faith or morals, such as the Church's opposition to contraception or homosexual life-styles, or the discipline of priestly celibacy, as if we are politicians who can be pressured to change a political policy!

Let me be clear here, Church teaching is not the opinion of the Pope and bishops that can be changed by lobbying or through the succession of a new Pope or Bishop, but the teaching of Jesus Christ, Son of God, safe-guarded and preserved by the teaching office of the Church.

My heart goes out to all those who have become trapped in this unhappy state of doubt and discontent, to which we can all become vulnerable at one time or another. I pray for their enlightenment by the Spirit of truth and love.

I, like many others, am aware of the enormous socio-cultural pressures, exerted through the media, culture and politics, that propagate secularism and relativism which fuel dissent and indifferentism within the Church. As the people of God we must develop strategies and counter-measures to protect ourselves from forces that are destructive of faith.

8.6   Right to the Purity and Integrity of the Faith

As bishop I am concerned that those in positions of responsibility pass on a full and complete exposition of Catholic doctrine. It is my duty to ensure that none are deprived of the right 'to receive the message of the Church in its purity and integrity and not to be disturbed by a particular dangerous opinion'. (CDF, *Instruction on the Ecclesial Vocation of the Theologian*, 37).

Dei Verbum sets up a series of checks and balances that should be used by theologians in studying scripture and by the faithful to judge the authenticity of sensational claims and media-hyped speculations:

Firstly, the Bible is the Book of the Church. In order for the meaning of the sacred texts to be correctly brought to light, 'the living tradition of the whole Church must be taken into account along with the harmony which exists between elements of the faith'. (*DV* 12).

Secondly, the Bible has been entrusted to the Church. The Church has final judgement over the interpretation of Scripture, 'which carries out the divine commission and ministry of guarding and interpreting the word of God'. (*DV* 12).

As Pope John Paul II puts it, a Catholic does not take an individualistic approach to Scripture, based on the assumption that they can be better understood outside the community of believers. The opposite is true, Scripture has been entrusted to the Church, 'in order to nourish faith and guide the life of charity.' (His Holiness Pope John Paul II, *Address on The Interpretation of the Bible in the Church*, 10).

In fact being part of the community of the Church is essential to truly understand Scripture. As Pope Benedict XVI puts it,

> Scripture requires exegesis, and it requires the context of the community in which it came to birth and in which it is lived. This is where its unity is to be found, and here too its unifying meaning is opened up. To put it yet another way: there are dimensions of meaning in the word and in words which only come to light within the living community of this history-generating word. (Pope Benedict XVI, *Address to representatives of culture*, France, September 2008).

Thirdly, the Bible cannot interpret itself. The deeper understanding of sacred Scripture is not to be undertaken solely through the historical critical method, but also through attention to the content and unity of the whole of Scripture (*DV* 12), and through the study of the Fathers of the Church and sacred liturgies (*DV* 23).

I propose the following for consideration and action by Catholics:

✓ The faithful have the right to a pure and whole faith, therefore under no circumstances are novel ideas or speculations to be promulgated from the pulpit or in the classroom.

✓ I ask all of you to assess the Catholic journals you subscribe to with this question in mind: do they consistently promote criticism and dissent from the teachings and discipline of the Catholic Church? If they do, please consider cancelling your subscription or, at least, do not make them available at the back of church.

✓ I would expect clergy, chaplains and RE specialists to keep themselves up to date with the thinking of the Church, through studying magisterial documents, particularly papal encyclicals, statements from the Congregation for the Doctrine of the Faith - and other appropriate Dicasteries - and from your own bishop.

8.7   The Authentic Approach to Inter-faith Dialogue

The emergence of a multi-cultural society with its diversity of world religions has raised questions about the relationship between Christian revelation and other religious traditions. The Second Vatican Council was ground-breaking in advocating dialogue and collaboration with the followers of other religions:

> The Church therefore, exhorts her sons, that through dialogue and collaboration with the followers of other religions, carried out with prudence and love and in witness to the Christian faith and life, they recognize, preserve and promote the good things, spiritual and moral, as well as the socio-cultural values found among these people. (*Nostra Aetate*, 2).

However, nowadays it is not uncommon to hear Catholics - misunderstanding the nature of inter-faith dialogue - describe Christianity as just one religious path among many. Often the metaphor of a journey up a mountain is used to describe the relationship between world religions. Christianity is described as just one path among many paths ascending the mountain, with all the religious paths converging on the cloud covered peak that represents the unfathomable, unknown reality of God.

The over-riding motivation behind this false understanding of dialogue appears to be a desire to reduce all religious belief to the same level, glossing over very real differences about the truth, in order to encourage co-operation and tolerance.

We need to return to the Council's understanding of dialogue between Christianity and other world religions if we are to remain true to the Catholic understanding of revelation.

> The Catholic Church rejects nothing that is true and holy in these religions. She regards with sincere reverence those ways of conduct and of life, those precepts and teachings which, though differing in many aspects from the ones she holds and sets forth, nonetheless often reflect a ray of that Truth which enlightens all people. Indeed, she proclaims, and ever must proclaim Christ, "the way the truth, and the life" (*Jn* 14,6), in whom people may find the fullness of religious life, in whom God has reconciled all things to Himself. (*Nostra Aetate*, 2).

Let's be clear here, the Council taught that Jesus Christ is the unique saviour of all humanity. The Church upholds what Jesus said of Himself, 'I am the way, and the truth, and the life. No one comes to the Father except through me.' (*Jn* 14:6). Jesus is not one religious leader among many, Christianity is not one type of revelation among many.

Without rejecting what is good and true in world religions, the Catholic Church upholds the truth that salvation is only found in Jesus Christ. (*Gaudium et Spes*, 10; *Ad Gentes*, 9)

> This Jesus is 'the stone that was rejected by you, the builders; it has become the cornerstone.' There is salvation in no one else, for there is no other name under heaven given among mortals by which we must be saved. (*Ac* 4:11-12).

How are we to understand the other world faiths? Other religions contain 'seeds of the divine Word' which the Church recognises with joy and respect. (*Ad Gentes*, 11; *Nostra aetate*, 2).

> 'Again, it is the Spirit who sows the 'seeds of the word' present in various customs and cultures, preparing them for full maturity in Christ… Whatever the Spirit brings about in human hearts and in the history of peoples, in cultures and religions, serves as a preparation for the Gospel and can only be understood in reference to Christ, the Word who took flesh by the power of the Spirit 'so that as perfectly human he would save all human beings and sum up all things'. (Congregation for the Doctrine of the Faith, *Dominus Iesus*, 12).

As Cardinal Ratzinger put it, all goodness and truth comes from the Father and are the word of the Holy Spirit. The seeds of the incarnate Word, Jesus Christ, are cast abroad everywhere. 'Yet we cannot shut our eyes to the *errors and illusions* that are present in these religions'. (Joseph Ratzinger, *Pilgrim Fellowship of Faith*, p 214).

In particular, we cannot shut our eyes to errors and illusions that are promulgated about the person of Jesus Christ in other religions.

I want to be clear here, I am a strong supporter of inter-faith dialogue that encourages co-operation and tolerance. We all have a duty to recognise and encourage what is true and good in other religions. However, we are doing a disservice to genuine dialogue if we water down what we know to be true about the uniqueness of Jesus Christ and His irreplaceable role in the salvation of all humanity. By insisting on Jesus' unique role we are definitely not claiming any superiority for ourselves or our behaviour, but the superiority of Jesus Christ, who is true God and true man.

> Indeed, God 'desires all men to be saved and come to the knowledge of the truth' (1 *Tm* 2:4); that is, God wills the salvation of everyone through the knowledge of the truth. Salvation is found in the truth. Those who obey the promptings of the Spirit of truth are already on the way of salvation. But the Church, to whom this truth has been entrusted, must go out to meet their desire, so as to bring them the truth. Because she believes in God's universal plan of salvation, the Church must be missionary. (*CCC*, 851).

8.8 Revelation - Objectives for the Renewal of the Church

8.8.1 Teach the Catholic Understanding of Revelation

Henri de Lubac characterises the authentic Catholic approach to revelation as maintaining a balance between two elements - revelation as the teaching of God and revelation as a personal relationship with God. It is generally recognised that the Second Vatican Council's document on revelation stresses revelation as the personal manifestation of God to counter-balance the First Vatican Council's stress on revelation as intellectual teaching.

> For this reason Jesus perfected revelation by fulfilling it through His whole work of making Himself present and manifesting Himself: through His words and deeds, His signs and wonders, but especially through His death and glorious resurrection from the dead and final sending of the Spirit of truth. (*DV* 4).

Unfortunately, since the close of the Council there has been a tendency in catechesis to interpret *Dei Verbum's* emphasis on revelation as personal relationship with God as supplanting the idea of revelation as the teaching of doctrinal truths. Granted, there had been an imbalance before the Council with faith reduced to a set of intellectual truths. However, now the imbalance has swung the other way with many Catholics viewing faith as merely the experience of a relationship with Jesus detached from definite doctrinal and moral truths.

As a consequence, it is true that there has been an over-emphasis on personal experience as the primary criterion in catechesis. As I wrote in *Fit for Mission? Schools*, there is a twofold problem with allowing personal experience rather than the content of God's self revelation to determine the teaching of the faith:

❖ First, no one can arrive at the whole truth on the basis of personal experience, because individual experience is isolated and limited (cf. Pope John Paul II, *Catechesi tradendae*, 22).

❖ Second, concentrating too much on the personal experience of people results in a failure to present the fullness of the faith or convey the whole sweep of God's unfolding love in Salvation History.

There has been a misguided assumption that 'experience' is guaranteed to be authentic and meaningful for the individual, but this makes the mistake of seeing 'experience' as something neutral. However, Pope Benedict XVI is surely right when he points out the danger of experience in a culture that promotes relativism:

> Relativism, by indiscriminately giving value to practically everything, has made "experience" all-important. Yet, experiences, detached from any consideration of what is good or true, can lead, not to genuine freedom, but to moral or intellectual confusion, to a lowering of standards, to a loss of self-respect, and even to despair. (Pope Benedict XVI, World Youth Day 2008).

The tragic consequence of an overemphasis on experience is that great truths of the faith tend to be ignored or treated superficially, such as: the mystery of the Most Holy Trinity; the incarnation of the Son of God; the virginal conception of Mary; Christ's real presence in the Eucharist.

The truth that must be insisted on in evangelisation and catechesis is that God invites us to enter into a friendly *dialogue* with Him, so that living among us through the sacraments, He can teach us the deepest truths about Himself and humankind, giving us the possibility of salvation.

> To our weak minds, to our weak hands, He entrusts His truth - the mystery of God the Father, the Son and the Holy Spirit; the mystery of God who "so loved the world that He gave His only Son" (*Jn* 3:16). He made us His friends - and how do we respond? ... Our redemption is brought about in this communion of wills: being friends of Jesus, to become friends of God. The more we love Jesus, the more we know Him, the more our true freedom develops and our joy in being redeemed flourishes. Thank you, Jesus, for your friendship! (*Homily of His Eminence Cardinal Joseph Ratzinger, during the Mass for the Election of the Roman Pontiff*, April 2005).

✓ I recommend that all clergy and catechists present revelation as the balance between the teachings of God and a personal relationship with God, as expressed in the *Catechism of the Catholic Church*.

✓ Therefore, the teaching of faith will always include, and go beyond, personal experience because we are dealing with the mystery of God.

✓ Catechesis must aim at the cultivation of a personal relationship with Christ, friend and teacher, so that one's personal life is interpreted and illuminated by the truths and data of the Catholic faith.

✓ An urgent demand of the times is that we encourage and foster members of the Catholic faithful to become apologists with the knowledge and courage to proclaim the rationality and beauty of our Catholic faith. The question of God's existence is again a popular topic due to polemical works from writers such as Richard Dawkins. This is a great opportunity to present the rationality of belief in God developed by the Church's natural theology tradition.

I would like interested parties and individuals to contact me with recommendations about how we develop this vital ministry in the Church.

I recommend the following works of Catholic apologetics:

• Fr Dwight Longenecker's *Christianity Pure and Simple* series of booklets published by Catholic Truth Society. Also, his *Adventures in Orthodoxy.*

• Peter Keeft and Ronald K. Tacelli, *Handbook of Christian Apologetics*, Intervasity Press, 1994.

• Mgr Ronald Knox, *The Beliefs of Catholics,* Ignatius Press, 2000.

- Patrick Madrid, *Where is that in the Bible?* Our Sunday Visitor, 2001.

- *Resources for Believing.* A series of pamphlets published by the Faith Movement.

- Barbara Reed Mason, *Is religion necessary & other questions?* Proclaim publications, 2007. Also, *A study guide for house groups on the Bible & in the light of the Compendium*, Proclaim publications.

8.8.2   The Joy of Meeting Christ through the *Catechism of the Catholic Church*

I'm sad to say that, on the whole, the *Catechism* has been ignored and side-lined, in catechesis and religious education in our diocese. My document, *Fit for Mission? Schools* and its ongoing implementation is an attempt to remedy this deficiency in the life of many of our schools.

Now I want to turn our attention to catechesis in the parishes, which the *Fit for Mission? Parish* review has revealed equally needs to be renewed through active and creative engagement with this wonderful, spirit-inspired teaching document that ensures the purity and integrity of the faith.

Why do so many clergy, catechists and teachers tend to dismiss out of hand the *Catechism of the Catholic Church*?

First of all, I think it is ignored due to a lack of knowledge about the *Catechism of the Catholic Church*. Surprising to say, some usually well-informed teachers in our Catholic schools think that when I am recommending the *Catechism* I mean the old *Penny Catechism*. They seem unaware of the publication of the English edition of the new *Catechism of the Catholic Church* nearly 14 years ago, in 1994!

Secondly, I suspect some people think they know better than the *Catechism of the Catholic Church*. Unfortunately, this is a consequence of the individualism and self-assertion that has infected some sections of the Church. Some people do not want - as they falsely see it - to be 'constrained' by precise definitions and teachings of faith and morals. Some people want to pick and choose what they believe, or don't believe, and so the whole idea of a catechism is irksome. The *Catechism* smacks of indoctrination to some who mistakenly feel that they themselves can make judgements about the content of faith. It is a great sadness to me that this attitude is not unknown among some priests, deacons, religious and laity.

8.8.2.1 It is Christ who teaches through the *Catechism*

Pope Benedict XVI describes the *Catechism* as bringing us anew the great gift of joy at meeting Jesus! In an age of scepticism and doubt, the *Catechism* trusts the biblical word, it trusts that the Gospels' portrayal of Jesus is truly the Jesus of history, allowing us to know Jesus again.

This sure and certain trust is the strength and value of the *Catechism* to catechesis because trust is the one thing necessary for a rich and living encounter between persons, between Jesus and ourselves. As Pope John Paul II puts it,

> At the heart of catechesis we find, in essence, a Person, the Person of Jesus of Nazareth, the only Son from the Father...To catechize is to reveal in the Person of Christ the whole of God's eternal design reaching fulfilment in that Person... Catechesis aims at putting people ...in communion...with Jesus Christ: only He can lead us to the love of the Father in the Spirit and make us share in the life of the Holy Trinity. (Pope John Paul II, *Catechesi tradendae*, 5.)

WHEN THE DISCIPLES SAW HIM WALKING ON THE SEA, THEY WERE TERRIFIED, SAYING, "IT IS A GHOST!' AND THEY CRIED OUT IN FEAR, BUT IMMEDIATELY JESUS SPOKE TO THEM AND SAID, "TAKE HEART, IT IS I; DO NOT BE AFRAID."

MATTHEW 14:26-27

At the heart of the *Catechism* we do not find an ideology or an 'official' Vatican theology, instead we truly encounter a person, the Person of Jesus Christ. As Pope John Paul II wrote in *Catechesi tradendae*, 'To catechize is to reveal in the Person of Christ the whole of God's eternal design reaching fulfilment in that Person' (*CCC* 426).

Through the *Catechism* - as a crystallisation of the Tradition of the Catholic Church and the Magisterium's interpretation of sacred Scripture - it is Christ who teaches us. When clergy or catechists use the *Catechism* in their ecclesial role as teachers of the faith, they enable 'Christ to teach with their lips'. Every clergyman or catechist should be able to apply to his or her self the words of Jesus, 'My teaching is not Mine, but His who sent Me'. (*CCC* 427).

It is for this reason that primacy must be given to *content* in catechesis because catechists have the duty of passing on the doctrines we have received from Christ, through His Church:

> Catechesis is not first and foremost a question of method, but of content, as the name itself indicates: it is about an organic presentation (*kat-echein*) of the whole of Christian revelation, in such a way as to make available to minds and hearts the word of him who gave his life for us. In this way, catechesis causes to resound within the heart of every human being a unique call that is ceaselessly renewed: "Follow me" (*Mt* 9:9). (Pope Benedict XVI, *Address to French Bishops*, France, September 2008)

✓ It is my hope that clergy will do their utmost to encourage members of their parishes to participate in training programmes for catechists, such as the *Echoes* catechists courses presented by Maryvale. I also encourage priests and deacons to enrol on these courses as part of their own on-going formation.

✓ I recommend the following commentaries on the *Catechism*:

Schönborn, Christoph, *Living the Catechism of the Catholic Church*. Ignatius Press, 2000 - A four volume commentary on the Four Pillars.

Ratzinger, Joseph & Schönborn, Christoph, *Introduction to the Catechism of the Catholic Church*. Ignatius Press, 1994 - a short guide to the Catechism from Pope Benedict XVI, the main architect of the Catechism.

✓ For guidance and ideas about using the Catechism in the parish, I recommend that you subscribe to the catechetical journal, *The Sower: The Teaching Journal for the Home, Parish and School.* Maryvale House, Maryvale Institute, Old Oscott Hill, Birmingham, B44 9BR.

✓ Willey, Petroc, Morgan, Barbara, & Morgan, Pierre, *The Catechism of the Catholic Church and the Craft of Catechesis*, Ignatius Press, 2008 - a useful book on how to use the Catechism in teaching, whether parish, school or the home.

8.8.3 Homilies Should Change Lives

Nothing can replace the liturgical homily as the most important moment of catechesis in the life of the parish. Priests and deacons, through Holy Orders, share in the bishop's teaching authority and ministry of the Word.

The Sunday homily is the summation of the pastor's relationship with Sacred Scripture. If the priest or deacon has an intimate, lively and passionate relationship with the Word of God, contained in Scripture and Tradition, then the homily will have the power to educate, enlighten and enthuse. Without this vital relationship, homilies often just become empty words, soon forgotten. As *Dei Verbum* puts it,

> Therefore, all the clergy must hold fast to the Sacred Scriptures through diligent sacred reading and careful study, especially the priests of Christ and others, such as deacons and catechists who are legitimately active in the ministry of the word. This is to be done so that none of them will become "an empty preacher of the word of God outwardly, who is not a listener to it inwardly" since they must share the abundant wealth of the divine word with the faithful committed to them, especially in the sacred liturgy. (*DV* 25).

It is my earnest hope that we will witness a renewal of homiletics, and I call on priests, deacons and laity to suggest to me ways we can develop and enrich this vital ministry of the word. I propose the following as good practice:

➤ Begin preparing the Sunday homily a week in advance, through meditation and prayer on the Scripture readings and prayers of the Mass. Ask oneself the question - what is the Lord trying to tell us? How does He want me to teach His word?

➤ Study the readings in their mutual relationship, using the Gospel as the key text to understand the others, as well as the liturgical season.

➤ Place Scripture at the heart of your daily life. Pope John Paul II used to take time out of his busy daily schedule to privately study and pray scripture.

➤ The Sunday homily should be neither too long, nor too short.

➤ The homily should never be omitted except for a serious reason on Sunday or holy days of obligation. (*SC* 52).

➤ The homily should be adapted to the needs of the hearers, addressing the concerns of life.

➤ Preaching and catechizing should be permeated with adoration and respect for the name of our Lord Jesus Christ. (*CCC* 2145).

The Synod on the Eucharist (2005) proposed that clergy establish the practise of thematic homilies that in the course of the liturgical year could address the great topics of the Christian faith: the Creed, the Our Father, the parts of the Mass, the Ten Commandments and other aspects of the faith. They also proposed that these thematic homilies should draw on the four pillars of the *Catechism of the Catholic Church*.

I recommend that priests and deacons set up similar schemes of catechetical homilies following the liturgical seasons. To those who may object that homilies cannot or should not be used for catechesis, I beg to differ, pointing to the example of St Augustine, one of the greatest preachers in the Catholic Church, who often used his homilies to catechize his congregations.

In 1993 John Cardinal O'Connor of New York launched a series of 41 homilies on the *Catechism of the Catholic Church*. He selected and commented on passages of the *Catechism* and meshed them with the Sunday readings from Sacred Scripture.

- John Cardinal O'Connor, *A Moment of Grace*, Ignatius Press, 1995.

8.8.4   Promote Devotion to the Martyrs of England and Wales

Truth means more than knowledge: knowing the truth leads us to discover the good. Truth speaks to the individual in his or her entirety, inviting us to respond with our whole being. This optimistic vision is found in our Christian faith because such faith has been granted the vision of the *Logos*, God's creative Reason, which in the Incarnation, is revealed as Goodness itself. Far from being just a communication of factual data - "informative" - the loving truth of the Gospel is creative and life-changing - "performative" (cf. *Spe Salvi* 2) (*Address of his Holiness Benedict XVI, Meeting with Catholic Educators*, Washington, April 2008).

I am sure that many of you will agree that we are living in a time which can be characterised as undergoing a crisis of truth. The very notion of truth is questioned as merely one opinion among many possible alternative opinions. I have met individuals who are in a state of 'paralysis' about making the choice of faith because, considering all religions as having equal worth, they cannot choose between the various claims to truth.

This is where the witness of the martyrs is invaluable in evangelisation and catechesis. Pope John Paul II called the martyrs the 'most authentic witnesses to the truth about existence.'

> The martyrs know that they have found the truth about life in the encounter with Jesus Christ, and nothing and no-one could ever take this certainty from them. Neither suffering nor violent death could ever lead them to abandon the truth which they have discovered in the encounter with Christ. (Pope John Paul II, *Fides et Ratio*, 32).

Pope John Paul II highlights how the martyrs witness to the life changing and creative nature of truth:

"LET ANYONE WITH EARS LISTEN!"

MATTHEW 13:9

➢ The witness of the martyrs continues to arouse interest, to draw agreement, to win a hearing and to invite emulation.

➢ From the moment they speak to us, we perceive it deep down as the truth we have sought for so long. The martyrs provide evidence of a love that has no need of lengthy arguments in order to convince.

➢ The martyrs stir in us a profound trust because they give voice to what we already feel and they declare what we would like to have the strength to express. (*Fides et Ratio*, 32).

We are truly blessed in this country with the example of the martyrs, those courageous witnesses to the truth of the Catholic faith.

✓ I would like to encourage a greater devotion to the martyrs , because I am very much aware of the truth of that ancient saying, 'The blood of the martyrs is the seed of the Church'. There is something deeply life-giving about the martyrs' witness to the truth that will benefit our witness to the truth.

✓ It would be good to organise processions and acts of witness throughout the land on the feast of the English Martyrs on or around 4th May.

8 Key Two: The Dogmatic Constitution on Divine Revelation

Areas for reflection	Suggested Actions

• How do I find out about and follow Church Tradition?
 	
• Am I aware of the difference between Tradition and traditions? What is essential to the identity of the Church and what is time-conditioned and changeable?
 	
• How do I develop strategies and counter-measures to protect myself from forces that are destructive of faith?
 	
• Do I indulge in speculations unsupported by proper reference to the teaching of the Catholic Church?
 	
• How do I cultivate a personal relationship with Christ through personal experience and the wealth of the Church's knowledge of Him contained in the teachings of God?
 	
• How do I ensure I actively engage with the homily?
 	
• How do I embrace with the so called *God question* so as to help our people know the reasonableness of belief in God and confront those who claim that God does not exist?
 	
• Do I harbour prejudice against other religions?
 	
• Am I racist?
	• Commit to a regular reading of a Catholic translation of the Bible.
	
	• Critically review any 'Catholic' journal you read to consider if they promote criticism and dissent from the teaching of the Catholic Church and consider whether you should continue to subscribe to them.
	
	• (Clergy, chaplains and RE specialists) Keep up to date by studying magisterial documents and statements from the Church.
	
	• Ensure you present revelation as a balance between the teachings of God and a personal relationship with God.
	
	• Consider whether you are called to become a faithful apologist with the knowledge and courage to proclaim the rationality and beauty of our Catholic Faith.
	
	• Contact the Bishop if you have ideas about how to develop apologists in our Diocese.
	
	• Consider reading the following:
	
	  • Fr Dwight Longenecker's *Christianity Pure and Simple* series of booklets published by Catholic Truth Society. Also, his *Adventures in Orthodoxy*
	
	  • Peter Keeft and Ronald K. Tacelli, *Handbook of Christian Apologetics*, Intervasity Press, 1994.
	
	  • Mgr Ronald Knox, *The Beliefs of Catholics*, Ignatius Press, 2000.
	
	  • Patrick Madrid, *Where is that in the Bible?* Our Sunday Visitor, 2001.
	
	  • *Resources for Believing.* A series of pamphlets published by the Faith Movement.

8 Key Two: The Dogmatic Constitution on Divine Revelation *(concluded)*	
Areas for reflection	**Suggested Actions**

	• Consider whether you should participate in the 'Echoes' catechists course and/or the Maryvale Catechists Course and/or the course in Evangelisation and Ministry in Parishes.
	
	 • Consider using the following to help in your enjoyment of the catechism:
	
	   • Schönborn, Christoph, *Living the Catechism of the Catholic Church*. Ignatius Press, 2000
	
	   • Ratzinger, Joseph & Schönborn, Christoph, *Introduction to the Catechism of the Catholic Church*. Ignatius Press, 1994.
	
	   • *The Sower: The Teaching Journal for the Home, Parish and School*. Maryvale Institute.
	
	   • Willey, Petroc, Morgan, Barbara, & Morgan, Pierre, *The Catechism of the Catholic Church and the Craft of Catechesis*, Ignatius Press, 2008.
	
	 • (Priests and Deacons) review 'good practise' in respect of homilies and implement.
	
	 • Consider a scheme of catechetical homilies following the liturgical seasons.
	
	 • Consider organising a procession and act of witness on the feast of the English Martyrs on or around 4th May.

9   Key Three: The Dogmatic Constitution on the Church

SUDDENLY FROM HEAVEN THERE CAME
A SOUND LIKE THE RUSH OF A VIOLENT
WIND, AND IT FILLED THE ENTIRE HOUSE
WHERE THEY WERE SITTING.

ACTS 2:2

KEY THREE:

THE DOGMATIC CONSTITUTION ON THE CHURCH

The Church. The Church derives from the praise and adoration of God. The proclamation and generous distribution of the incarnate Word, through Gospel and Eucharist, manifests our co-operation with God's love for all humankind.

I think it's true to say that *Lumen Gentium* has brought about the most profound and far-reaching changes to the way many Catholics view the Church and other churches and ecclesial communities. Slowly in Lancaster, through our Fit for Mission? review, some of us have begun to recognise and experience the Church as something within us - not as an institution outside us. (Joseph Ratzinger, *The Ecclesiology of Vatican II*).

The Church is not an institution devised and built by men ... but a living reality... It lives still throughout the course of time. Like all living realities it develops, it changes ... and yet in the very depths of its being it remains the same; its inmost nucleus is Christ... To the extent that we look upon the Church as organization ... like an association ... we have not yet arrived at a proper understanding of it. Instead, it is a living reality and our relationship with it ought to be - life. (Romano Guardini, *The Church of the Lord*).

We need to be clear here that Guardini and Ratzinger are not advocating individualistic subjectivism towards the Church. The Church that is awakening in our hearts is always the apostolic Church instituted among the Twelve Apostles, founded on St Peter and handed on to the Pope and the bishops. The Church awakening in our hearts is always historical, objective and scriptural.

The restoration of the centrality of biblical images of the Church in *Lumen Gentium* are an expression of this great truth - the Church is the divine life within us - expressed in the images of the Church as the *Sacrament of Salvation*, the *People of God*, and the *Body of Christ*.

Reflecting on *Lumen Gentium* 20 years later, the Extraordinary synod of bishops (1985) concluded that 'much was done by the Second Vatican Council so that the Church as communion might be more clearly understood and concretely incorporated into life.' (Extraordinary Synod, *Final Report*).

Lumen Gentium's presentation of the biblical images of the Church tells us four things about the inner nature of the Church as communion:

> ➤ The multiplicity of images indicates that the Church shares in the inexpressible mystery of divine communion. No one image in itself is sufficient to convey this.

> ➤ The Church is the creation of God, not man, who unites humanity through His indwelling in them as individuals and as a people.

> ➤ The Church is an institution that grows in the world like a seed, its growth and history are part of the growth and history of the world.

> ➤ The Church is a many-sided communion whose inner force is Christ and the Holy Spirit expressed through an 'organ of unity' - the eucharist, hierarchy and charisms. (Grillmeier in Herbert Vorgrimler, *Commentary on the Documents of Vatican II*, p.144).

9.1 The Church is a Sign of Communion with Christ and each Other

As Cardinal Ratzinger puts it so beautifully, 'Christ is present in our hearts and it is there that Christ forms His Church':

> The Church grows from within and moves outwards, not vice-versa. Above all, she is the sign of the most intimate communion with Christ. She is formed primarily in a life of prayer, the sacraments and the fundamental attitudes of faith, hope and love. Thus if someone should ask what must I do to become Church and to grow like the Church, the reply must be: you must become a person who lives faith, hope and charity. What builds the Church is prayer and the communion of the sacraments; in them the prayer of the Church comes to meet us. (Cardinal Ratzinger, *The Ecclesiology of Vatican II*).

Through the incarnation the Son of God took a *body*, and through the gift of the Holy Spirit at Pentecost He continues to take a *body*, the Church. The essential point to grasp here is that Christ gives Himself only in His historical body - the Church - and never as a pure ideal that can be grasped by the solitary individual.

> Christ has formed a body for Himself. If I want to find Him and make Him mine, I am directly called to become a humble and complete and full member of His Body, and, by becoming one of His members, becoming an organ of his Body in this world, I will be so for eternity. (Cardinal Ratzinger, *The Ecclesiology of Vatican II*).

Lumen Gentium also uses the image of the Church as the *People of God* to convey the active, historical nature of the Church as the sign of the communion with Christ and each other. God's salvific actions in history are directed towards the formation of a 'community of salvation' (*LG* 9). This history follows a rocky and sometimes scandalous path due to the sinful, obdurate, fallen nature of humanity. As Cardinal Dulles puts it, the image of the Church as the people of God, 'allows for a greater distance between the Church and its divine head'. (Avery Dulles, *Models of the Church*, p. 53).

The image of a motley group of people moving through history towards the end of time, also enables recognition of the variety of ways in which communion exists to the Church, allowing the events of the Great Schism with the East and the Protestant Reformation to be recognised as part of the history of Christ's body.

9.2 Five Major Developments

Lumen Gentium's great achievement has been the implementation of five major developments that serve the Church as a communion with Christ and each other:

- ❖ Both *Lumen Gentium* and its application in *Unitatis Redintegratio* reflect a paradigm shift in the Catholic Church's attitude to other Christian churches and ecclesial communities based on the acknowledgement that faith, hope and charity 'can exist outside the visible boundaries of the Catholic Church' (*UR* 3; cf. *LG* 8). As a consequence, there has been a growth in ecumenical relationships between the Catholic Church and the world's family of Christians.

- ❖ *Lumen Gentium* marks the recovery of the sense of the community or college of bishops, based on the idea that apostolic succession isn't just the individual link between a bishop and the apostles, but the idea that being a bishop is more importantly about being united with other bishops who, as a body, are in succession to the apostles. This has resulted in the strengthening of the identity and role of the individual bishop, and the college of bishops, in union with their head, the Pope, in the life of the Church.

- ❖ The Council Fathers restored the permanent diaconate in order to develop the Church's exercise of 'charity in the performance of social or charitable works' (*Ad gentes*, 16). The purpose of re-establishing permanent deacons is at the service of the *koinonia* [communion] of the Church, as Pope Benedict XVI puts it, 'As a community, the Church must practise love. Love needs to be organised if it is to be an ordered service to the community' (*Deus Caritas Est*, 20). After an extensive study and review of the Permanent Diaconate, I hope to produce *Fit for Mission? Diaconate*.

❖ *Lumen Gentium* also sought to strengthen the vocation of the laity. The Council did much to clarify the rights and responsibilities of the laity to enable them to take a more active part in the life of the Church, particularly in worship, the mission of the Church and their particular calling to proclaim the Gospel in the secular sphere, the area of their competence. The Council set this portrayal of the vocation of the laity in the context of the universal call to holiness.

❖ Recognising that the Church is the sacramental sign of salvation, the Council Fathers also gave attention to the visible government of the Church through the promotion of Episcopal Conferences as national agencies of communion for the local Church, and the role of synods to express the collegial nature of the episcopacy.

9.3 Threats to the Communion of the Church

Despite these great and praise worthy achievements resulting from *Lumen Gentium*, we have witnessed over the past forty years a growing crisis in the Catholic understanding or self-identity of the Church. While still Cardinal Ratzinger, Pope Benedict XVI identified the crisis about the idea of Church as lying at the root of all other crises that face us. He proposes that this crisis consists of a number of elements:

➤ The authentically Catholic meaning of 'Church' is disappearing.

➤ Many no longer believe that the Church is a reality willed by the Lord Himself.

➤ The Church is increasingly being viewed as a human construct, an instrument created by us that can be freely re-organised according to pragmatic need.

➤ Catholics are forgetting that behind the exterior, human reality of the Church, there is a fundamental, more-than-human structure and reality willed by God Himself, which is therefore inviolable.

➤ If the Church is viewed as a human construct, the product of our own efforts, then even the contents of faith assume an arbitrary character and are thrown into question. (Joseph Ratzinger, *The Ratzinger Report*, p. 45-46).

"COME TO ME, ALL YOU THAT ARE WEARY AND ARE CARRYING HEAVY BURDENS, AND I WILL GIVE YOU REST".

MATTHEW 11:28

As a result of this *a priori* assumption that the fundamental structures of the Church are nothing more than the product of sociological and psychological forces, and not a supernatural reality willed by God, a wide-range of threats to the mystery of the Church's authentic communion have emerged.

9.4   The Threat to Genuine Ecumenism

Those of us that can remember the time when Catholics were forbidden to attend services held by non-Catholic Christians, including the funerals of friends, or even pray together, will still rejoice at the convivial relationships that have grown up between the Catholic Church and other Christian communities in this country. It is an event as historically significant as the fall of the Berlin wall.

However, it has been regrettable to have observed in responses to our *Fit for Mission? Parish* review that in certain circles the Catholic understanding of the Church is being blurred over and even dropped due to a misplaced egalitarianism and premature urge to gloss over significant differences. Some Catholics are in danger of forgetting the uniqueness of the Catholic Church and its irreplaceable role in salvation history.

Yes, we are 'churches' together in the sense of sometimes working together, sometimes praying together, and sometimes serving society together, but this cannot obscure the fact that we are not, yet, in full communion. We are together, and we are also not yet together. To misunderstand the limitations of our 'togetherness' or pretend otherwise is a threat to genuine ecumenism. It is a sad truth to have to admit that we are almost doctrinally as far apart as ever.

We must also guard against the temptation to dilute or drop doctrines of the Catholic Church out of a misplaced zeal to promote the illusion of unity between Christians, such as the Marian dogmas. As Pope Benedict XVI puts it,

> We must guard against any temptation to view doctrine as divisive and hence an impediment to the seemingly more pressing and immediate task of improving the world in which we live. In fact, the history of the Church demonstrates that praxis is not only inseparable from, but actually flows out of *didache* or teaching. The more closely we strive for a deeper understanding of the divine mysteries, the more eloquently our works of charity will speak of God's bountiful goodness and love towards all. (Pope Benedict XVI, World Youth Day 2008).

For example, a true understanding of the dogma of the Assumption of the Blessed Virgin Mary will help us more appreciate the value God places on physical bodiliness and the material world, with implications for Christian involvement in environmental issues.

9.5   The Genuine Understanding of Communion

Cardinal Dulles writes that until the Second Vatican Council, the common Catholic position was that divine and salvific faith did not exist among members of other Christian communities. (Avery Dulles, *The Craft of Theology*, p. 179). As already stated, both *Lumen Gentium* (*LG*) and *Unitatis Redintegratio* (*UR*) reflect a paradigm shift based on the acknowledgement that faith, hope and charity 'can exist outside the visible boundaries of the Catholic Church' (*UR* 3; cf. *LG* 8). The use of the formulas *subsistit in* [subsists] and *elementa Ecclesiae* [elements of the Church] in *Lumen Gentium* was crucial in allowing this ecumenical breakthrough.

The Ecclesiology of Communion is fundamental to Vatican II's maintenance of the oneness of the Church of Christ, while at the same time allowing positive recognition of non-Catholic churches and communities.

> **Definition. Ecclesiology of communion:** This means an ecclesiology which defines the Church as an organic whole composed of spiritual bonds (faith, hope and charity), and of visible structural forms (the profession of faith, the sacramental economy, the pastoral ministry), and which culminates in the Eucharistic mystery, the source and expression of the unity of the Church, or rather of the one Church. Each of these elements is considered in so far as it promotes, conditions, realises or brings about 'communion' which is the Church. (Herbert Vorgrimler, *Commentary on the Documents of Vatican II*, vol. 2. p. 64.)

Lumen Gentium and *Unitatis Redintegratio* employ the ecclesiology of communion to harmonize two doctrinal statements:

1. That the Church of Christ, despite Christian disunity, 'continues to exist fully only in the Catholic Church' [*subsistit in*];

2. There exist elements of sanctification and truth in churches and ecclesial communities not yet in full communion with the Catholic Church [*elementa Ecclesia*] (cf. *LG* 15 & *UR* 3).

9.6 The Church of Christ Subsists in the Catholic Church

> Christ, the one Mediator, established and ceaselessly sustains here on earth His holy Church, the community of faith, hope and charity, as a visible structure... This Church, constituted and organised in the world as a society, subsists in the Catholic Church, which is governed by the successor of Peter and by the bishops in union with that successor... (*LG* 8).

There has been some confusion about the exact meaning of the phrase, 'the Church of Christ subsists in the Catholic Church'. Let's be clear, it does not mean that the Church of Christ exists in its fullness anywhere else. It does mean that the one Church of Christ received by the apostles continues to exist fully in the Catholic Church - in all the fullness of its oneness, holiness, catholicity and apostolicity.

As the Congregation for the Doctrine of the Faith explained in its recent *Responses to Some Questions Regarding Certain Aspects of the Doctrine of the Church* (2008),

'Christ "established here on earth" only one Church and instituted it as a "visible and spiritual community", that from its beginning and throughout the centuries has always existed and will always exist, and in which alone are found *all* the elements that Christ Himself instituted... This Church, constituted and organised in this world as a society, subsists in the Catholic Church, governed by the successor of Peter and the Bishops in communion with him'.

Consequently, it is through the Catholic Church alone that *full* incorporation into the body of Christ can take place, and that the whole unity of the Church is guaranteed. The unity of the Church is manifested in the *communio* of the bishops under the Pope, and through the sacrament of unity, the Eucharist.

9.7   Elements of the Church outside the Catholic Church

Full incorporation into the communion of the Church depends on full sacramental life and unity regulated by the office of Peter and the Apostles. However, it must be recognised that Christian communities outside the Catholic Church are used by the Holy Spirit as the means of salvation for their members (*UR* 3), through what they hold in common with the Catholic Church.

> Moreover, some and even very many of the significant elements and endowments which together go to build up and give life to the Church itself, can exist outside the visible boundaries of the Catholic Church: the written word of God; the life of grace; faith, hope and charity, with the other interior gifts of the Holy Spirit, and visible elements too. (*UR* 3).

Pope John Paul II develops the significance of 'Ecclesial elements' in his encyclical *Ut Unum Sint*, further recognising the ecclesial character of non-Catholic communities:

> Indeed, the elements of sanctification and truth present in the other Christian communities, in a degree which varies from one to the other, constitute the objective basis of the communion, albeit imperfect, which exists between them and the Catholic Church. To the extent that these elements are found in other Christian communities, *the one church of Christ is effectively present in them*. (Pope John Paul II, *Ut Unum Sint*)

The idea that the more that is held in common, the more Christians are in communion is reflected in the distinction that *Unitatis Redintegratio* makes between churches and ecclesial communities. At the heart of this distinction is the principle that the Eucharist and apostolic succession are so essential to the nature of the Church that a community cannot be called a 'church' when there are doubts about the existence of the full reality of these elements.

I draw the following conclusions for the ecumenical life of Catholics that is so close to my heart and expressed as one of the urgent Mission Priorities in the *Final Proposals* of the *Fit for Mission? Parish* review:

✓ I consider it important that all Catholics clearly grasp the Second Vatican Council's understanding that there is one Church of Christ, not many churches. While the Catholic Church possesses the fullness of communion, non Catholic churches and communities participate, to various degrees, in the communion of the one Church of Christ.

Such an appreciation is essential to maintaining our distinct and definite identity, which is not about encouraging separateness but about maintaining the truth of things. True friends are able to speak the truth together.

Each one of us should be ready and able to give a clear exposition of the Catholic understanding of the Church, and avoid formulations, expressions or behaviour that might give rise to error and misunderstanding.

✓ I recommend that everyone should actively engage in the vital work of genuine ecumenism, through prayer and engagement, while at the same time maintaining the full Catholic understanding of the Church as a communion, based on the Eucharist and apostolic succession.

I invite you to consider the following questions:

❖ Do you have a Catholic understanding of the Church?

❖ Do you consider the Catholic Church unique, or just one church among many churches?

❖ Do you look on non Catholic churches and communities as variously participating in the communion of the one Church of Christ?

❖ Do you value the distinct spiritualities and traditions of other non Catholic churches?

9.8 The Threat to Full Communion in the Church

As indicated earlier, one of the great changes brought about by the Second Vatican Council that strengthened the communion of the Church has been the renaissance of the role of the Bishop and the body of Bishops under the headship of the Pope. As Pope John Paul II puts it, the unity of the episcopacy is one of the constitutive elements of the communion of the Church. (Pope John Paul II, *Apostolos Suos*, 8).

"I DO NOT CALL YOU SERVANTS ANY LONGER, BECAUSE THE SERVANT DOES NOT KNOW WHAT THE MASTER IS DOING; BUT I HAVE CALLED YOU FRIENDS, BECAUSE I HAVE MADE KNOWN TO YOU EVERYTHING THAT I HAVE HEARD FROM MY FATHER".

JOHN 15:15

This unity of the episcopacy has its origins in the will of the Lord, in that 'just as St Peter and the other apostles constituted one apostolic college, so in a similar way the Roman Pontiff as the successor of Peter and the bishops as the successors of the apostles are joined together'. (*LG* 22).

Since the Council, this collegial spirit has found expression in national Episcopal

Conferences (*LG* 23) such as the Catholic Bishops Conference of England and Wales. The Extraordinary Synod (1985) welcomed the existence of such conferences, stating, 'No one can doubt their pastoral utility, indeed their necessity in the present situation.' (Extraordinary Synod, *Final Report*).

I feel that I must share my thoughts on national Episcopal Conferences because our deliberations and decisions as bishops influence the life of the national church and impact the lives of most of the Catholics in my diocese.

The Extraordinary Synod (1985) went on to highlight an area of concern about the conferences, that they must keep in mind the 'inalienable responsibility of each bishop in relation to the universal Church and the particular Church'. Pope John Paul II's apostolic letter *Apostolos Suos* further sought to highlight the necessity of limiting the authority of national Episcopal conferences, along with conference committees, commissions, advisors and experts in favour of the authority of the individual bishop in his diocese and through the bishop's direct and personal co-operation in a national conference.

I must admit that during my nearly 15 years as a bishop I have increasingly come to share certain concerns about the relationship between individual bishops and the National Conference:

> ➤ Due to the division of areas of responsibility among the bishops, such as education, liturgy, healthcare etc, there can often be reluctance among the rest of the bishops to speak out on these issues, as if somehow they had handed over their competence in these areas to the responsible bishop and his particular committee. For example, there seemed some surprise in some circles that I had issued my teaching document, *Fit for Mission? Schools*.

> ➤ I must register, too, my disappointment that our Bishops' Conference recently could not agree a collegial response to the Government's legislation on same-sex adoption.

> ➤ The problem with attempting to arrive at a consensus among bishops with, sometimes, divergent views, is statements and documents from Episcopal Conferences have a tendency to be often flat and 'safe' at a time when we need passionate and courageous public statements that dare to speak the full truth in love. The effort to achieve a consensus results - as Cardinal Ratzinger so aptly expressed it - often in the loss of the 'scandal' and the 'folly' of the Gospel, so that we are no longer the 'salt' and 'leaven' so urgently needed. (Cardinal Ratzinger, *The Ratzinger Report*, p. 62).

> ➤ Agencies and Commissions of national conferences must surely uphold the fullness of the Church's teaching, particularly doctrinal and moral teaching, in their collaboration with secular agencies. I'm thinking in particular of agencies with a responsibility for education or economic development. The staff of these agencies are often in a position to witness to the truth of the Church's teaching on,

say, the theology of the body with its positive refutation of pre-marital sex, 'safe sex', or artificial birth control, in their dealings with government departments and committees. There must be no back-peddling on these issues just because certain truths are unwelcome in the corridors of power.

➤ Sometimes the Secretariats of Episcopal Conferences forget that they are the servants of the bishops, and so their staff take it upon themselves to decide what is best, i.e. setting the agendas of conference meetings. It needs to be re-iterated that bishops have not delegated their authority to the committees and staff of Catholic bishops' conferences.

➤ In Anthony Howard's official biography of Cardinal Basil Hume, he writes that his Eminence left behind a 'semi-autonomous Church'. (Anthony Howard, *Basil Hume*, p. 321). Leaving aside the question of the truth or otherwise of this observation, I think it succinctly identifies the danger inherent in the workings of national episcopal conferences. We must guard against the Catholic Church degenerating into local churches who consider themselves almost autonomous in some respects from the See of Rome.

➤ It is not acceptable for us to dismiss documents issued from Roman Dicasteries, saying, 'That's for others, not for us! We don't have that problem here'. Such an attitude can sometimes result in documents and statements from the Holy Father's Dicasteries not being given the serious attention they require. There must be an active dialogue between the local church and the Holy See.

➤ We must never forget that for each local church to be fully Church, there must be present in it the supreme authority of the Church: the Episcopal College *together with their head, the Supreme Pontiff, and never apart from him*. As the Congregation for the Doctrine of the Faith puts it, 'we must see the ministry of the Successor of Peter, not only as a 'global' service, reaching each particular Church from 'outside', as it were, but as belonging already to the essence of each particular Church from 'within' '. (CDF, *Letter to the Bishops of the Catholic Church on Some Aspects of the Church Understood as Communion*, 13).

9.9 The Need for Confident and Courageous Bishops

I am convinced that there is a need for Bishops to re-exercise their individual teaching charism:

> [Bishops] are authentic teachers, that is, teachers endowed with the authority of Christ, who preach to the people committed to them the faith they must believe and put into practice... Bishops, teaching in communion with the Roman Pontiff, are to be revered by all as witnesses to divine and Catholic truth. (*LG* 25).

We must keep it clearly in mind that the Bishop is not the manager of his local branch of the Catholic Church, who reports to the board of the national Episcopal Conference.

Rather the Bishop is 'a visible source and foundation of the unity of the particular Church entrusted to his pastoral ministry' (*LG* 23).

The presence of confident, courageous and prophetic bishops is vital for the well-being of the Church during this time of increasingly aggressive secularism. We need to remind ourselves of the authority and dignity of bishops:

❖ Bishops preside in the place of God over the flock whose shepherds they are, as teachers of doctrine, priests of sacred worship and ministers of government.

❖ By divine institution, Bishops have succeeded to the Apostles as Shepherds of the Church.

❖ Bishops govern the particular churches entrusted to them as the vicars and ambassadors of Christ, by their counsel, exhortations and example, but also by their authority and sacred power. (Pope John Paul, *Apostolos Suos*, 19).

I conclude the following as being vital for the life of our diocese:

➢ Bishops need the wholehearted support and fraternal obedience of priests if they are to witness to the truth of the gospel.

➢ Bishops need the self-forgetful service and humble obedience of permanent deacons if they are to serve suffering humanity.

➢ Bishops need the loyalty, engagement and receptive obedience of the laity if they are to inspire the transformation of the world.

➢ Bishops must always be open to, and draw upon, the competencies and insights of the laity, religious and clergy.

➢ In order to ensure that our dioceses are fully Church, it is important that the Petrine element of our local Church is expressed in two ways: firstly, through praying for the Holy Fathers intentions, and secondly, through attentive engagement with documents and statements from the Vatican, by diocesan commissions, parishes, schools and Catholic households.

9.10   The Church - Objectives for the Renewal of the Church

9.10.1 True Catechesis into Communion with Christ and His Church

"The definitive aim of catechesis is to put people not only in touch, but also in communion and intimacy, with Jesus Christ"...Communion with Jesus Christ, by its own dynamic, leads the disciple to unite himself with everything with which Jesus Christ Himself was profoundly united: with God his Father, who sent Him into the world, and with the Holy Spirit, who impelled His mission; with the Church, His body, for which He gave Himself up, with mankind and with His brothers whose lot He wished to share. (*General Directory for Catechesis*, 81).

Last year I issued *Fit for Mission? Schools* to renew evangelisation and catechesis within our schools and colleges. How far has its vision of catechesis been received in my own diocese, and wider afield? Is its hope of changing the practice of catechesis being realised?

Everyone knows that there is an urgent need for Catholics to know and live their faith better, everyone knows that the practice of catechesis needs to be developed throughout Church in this country, but yet there is no great passion for the enterprise. What needs to happen is for catechesis to take hold of the heart and imagination of thousands. If people saw catechesis as another word for attaining a deeper relationship, deeper personal knowledge, a deeper communion with Jesus, the passion, the fire would catch in many hearts. True catechesis is profoundly personal and transforming, through which the Church awakens in our souls!

To fulfil its task, catechesis employs two principal means: the power of the Gospel message and the joy of Christian life:

9.10.1.1   The Power of the Gospel Message

Simply put, catechesis is about the Church sharing her desire to know Christ more fully, and understand Him better, her longing to make Him present, to more closely walk in His footsteps, and to learn to pray with Him. The Church transmits the faith which she herself lives:

- ❖ Her understanding of the mystery of God and His salvific plan.

- ❖ The wonder of God's invitation in Jesus to us to share His divine life and work.

- ❖ Her vision of man's highest vocation, measured by the stature of Christ, and Christ-like saints.

- ❖ The style of evangelic life which communicates the joy of the Kingdom, and it's imperative for self-giving love and justice.

- ❖ The hope which pervades her and animates her engagement with a fallen world.

- ❖ The love which she has for humanity and all God's creatures.

9.10.1.2   The Joy of Christian Life

Also, in this age of assertive individualism it is necessary to develop catechesis as an education in community life, in order to break-through the common attitude of 'consuming' liturgy and events in the parish as if they were just another provision from the service sector! I have been made aware through submissions to our *Fit for Mission? Parish* review that increasingly Catholics 'shop around' to find the Mass and parish that most fits in with their life-style and tastes.

The General Directory for Catechesis (GDC, 86) outlines the Christ-like attitudes that catechesis should aim to inculcate:

- ❖ The spirit of simplicity and humility.

- ❖ Solicitude for the least among the brethren.

- ❖ Particular care for those who are alienated.

- ❖ Fraternal correction.

- ❖ Common prayer.

- ❖ Mutual forgiveness.

- ❖ Fraternal love.

- ✓ I recommend that every parish or deanery establishes a 'Communion with Christ' group to plan and present catechetical programmes that facilitate deeper communion with Christ and deeper Christ-like communion with each other. It is important not to lose sight of these goals for our catechetical programmes. These are the bench marks against which they should be frequently measured. If they are not working, try something else!

- ✓ As a start, I recommend the CTS *Evangelium* programme - adult catechesis for parishes, based on the four pillars of the *Catechism of the Catholic Church* - Profession of Faith, Sacraments, Moral Life and Prayer.

9.10.2 New Movements - Living in a Time of Spiritual Renaissance

The history of the Church appears to oscillate between periods of spiritual renaissance and periods of spiritual decline and hopelessness. The Church swings on a wide arc between Pentecost and Gethsemane. Looking around at today's Church I think that though we have swung into a time of Gethsemane, I can see signs of us swinging back towards Pentecost. There are definite indications of an incipient spiritual renaissance even within Britain.

As indicated in my earlier section, 'a time of confidence and communion', since the Second Vatican Council the New Movements and religious orders have emerged in the Church. Two hundred international groups and communities, comprising lay people, religious, priests, deacons and bishops, have grown up alive with charisms of the Holy Spirit, and with a passion to live out the gospel in new ways in modern society. Though not all have survived, they showed, if even for a short time, great hope.

It may be said that the Vatican Council marked the Church's re-discovery of her charismatic nature.

> [The Holy Spirit] furnishes and directs [the Church] with various gifts, both hierarchical and charismatic, and adorns her with the fruits of His grace'.(*LG* 4).
>
> '[The Holy Spirit] distributes special graces among the faithful of every rank. By these gifts He makes them fit and ready to undertake various tasks and offices for the renewal and building up of the Church... Whether these charisms be very remarkable or more simple and widely diffused, they are to be received with thanksgiving and consolation since they are fitting and useful for the needs of the Church'. (*LG* 12).

✓ We would, indeed, be foolish not to avail ourselves of the bountiful generosity of the Holy Spirit, and so I hope that across the diocese that we will offer a hospitable welcome to the new movements and new religious orders.

✓ I am aware that our policy of hospitality towards new movements may come at the cost of possible tensions between them and the local parishes. There is always a shock and adjustment associated with the new. I ask that the parishes be courageous and patient, and the new movements be sensitive and open-handed - in all things, a communion based on charity!

Key Three: The Dogmatic Constitution on the Church	
Areas for reflection	**Suggested Actions**
• Do I have a Catholic understanding of the Church? • Do I consider the Catholic Church unique, or just one church among many churches? • Do I look on non-Catholic churches and communities as variously participating in the communion of the one Church of Christ? • Do I value the distinct spiritualities and traditions of other non Catholic churches? • How do I view 'new movements' in the Church?	• Pray for the Holy Father's intentions. • Undertake attentive engagement with documents and statements from the Vatican (diocesan commissions, parishes, schools and Catholic households). • Establish a 'Communion with Christ' group to plan and present catechetical programmes. • Undertake the CTS *Evangelium* programme.

10 Key Four: The Pastoral Constitution on the Church in the Modern World

WHEN HE SAW HIM, HE WAS MOVED WITH PITY. HE WENT TO HIM AND BANDAGED HIS WOUNDS

LUKE 10:33–34

KEY FOUR:

THE PASTORAL CONSTITUTION ON THE CHURCH IN THE MODERN WORLD

Mission: The Church carries the light of love received from God out into the world, taking it into all the dark places of injustice and suffering in the knowledge that the light came into the world and darkness could not overcome it.

Watching the coverage of Pope Benedict XVI's magnificent pastoral visit to the United States in April 2008, one image remains with me that captures - to my mind - the long-lasting impact of *Gaudium et Spes* on the life of the Church - the image of the Holy Father walking across the Assembly Hall of the United Nations, and addressing the representatives of the world's nations - like Pope Paul VI and Pope John Paul II before him - as the successor of St Peter, the Vicar of Christ.

Standing before the nations of the world, the Holy Father came in a spirit of dialogue and witness to the transcendent truth of humanity, embodying in his person the impulse that shaped *Gaudium et Spes* - the pastoral imperative of dialogue with the world in order to safeguard the full nature and rights of humanity. As Yves Congar puts it, this pastoral approach, 'intends to present the truth of salvation in a way which is close to men and women of today and which accepts their difficulties and tries to answer their questions'. (Yves Congar in Alberic Stacpoole's, *Vatican II Revisited By Those Who Were There*, p. 347).

Pope Benedict XVI's address at the UN distils the essence of the Church's approach to the world since the Second Vatican Council: The Church is committed to contributing her experience 'of humanity' in order to attain freedom for every believer and increase the protection given to the rights of the person. 'Those rights are grounded and shaped by the transcendent nature of the person'. (Address of His Holiness Benedict XVI, *Meeting with the Members of the General Assembly of the United Nations Organisation*, 18th April 2008).

One of the Mission Priorities of the *Final Proposals* of our *Fit for Mission? Parish* review expresses the same approach: 'Develop mission with Faith & Justice and environmental issues - seeing it as an integral part of Catholic life'.

First, the Church *offers* her experience of humanity to the world, she does not seek to *impose* it. Second, the Church offers her rich experience of humanity in order to protect the recognition of a dimension of human nature that is in danger of being overlooked - the transcendent, spiritual nature of man. Third, the Church seeks to convince the world that recognition of the full humanity of the person is the only guarantee of human rights, and is the condition for 'humanity's hope for a better world', because self-transcendence is the basis of peace, development and cooperation.

Gaudium et Spes also recognises that the Church benefits from the world's participation in dialogue with her. For the first time in the history of the Church an ecumenical council was able to recognise the great values of the world. As Henri de Lubac puts it, 'Nothing authentically human, whatever its origin, can be alien to her. The heritage of all peoples is her inalienable dowry. In her, man's desires and God's have their meeting-place'. (Henri de Lubac, *Catholicism*, p. 297).

10.1   What is the Church's Experience of Humanity?

Gaudium et Spes is itself a dialogue between the Christian and modern secular man on the fundamental questions presented by science and technology about who and what humanity really is. It maps out the light and shadows of human existence - the dignity of man set against the void of sin:

* **The Dignity of the Person**: unity, intellect, conscience, freedom, communion and adoration.

* **The Void of Sin**: division, relativism, utilitarianism, death, atheism, both individual and systematic.

10.2   Our Starting Point is the Human Person Made in the Image of God

The biblical understanding of the person created in the image and likeness of God (*Gn* 1:24) is the starting point of *Gaudium et Spes*. Creation is God's initiation of divine self-communication as man's fundamental reason to exist. Nowadays we often hear that man is nothing more than a superior animal, a naked ape! The biblical image of the person created in the image and likeness of God conveys our vocation to an authentic dignity and communion, because it expresses the capacity of man's inner-nature for God's self-communication.

Simply put, we are more than nature or nurture, because who we are deep down lies beyond the physical, beyond the realm of the senses. As *Gaudium et Spes* 14 puts it, 'For by his interior qualities he outstrips the whole sum of mere things. He plunges into the depths of reality whenever he enters into his own heart; God, Who probes the heart, awaits him there'.

The Council Fathers identify this basic experience of the person's spiritual nature with the possession of a 'spiritual and immortal soul'. The soul is 'that by which he is most especially in God's image' (*CCC* 363). Consequently, one of the truths that the modern world needs to hear from the Church's experience of humanity is that 'Man is a unity of body and soul' (*GS* 14). The body is a personal reality that shares in the dignity of 'the image of God', and is therefore more than matter, more than nerve endings to be endlessly gratified.

This is the origin of the dignity and excellence of our spiritual life in terms of our capacity for truth, goodness and freedom. It also sets freedom in a greater, more dignified context than the current impoverished preoccupation with freedom as assertive, self-gratification:

> Only in freedom can man direct himself toward goodness. Our contemporaries make much of this freedom and pursue it eagerly; and rightly to be sure. Often however they foster it perversely as a license for doing whatever pleases them, even if it is evil. For its part, authentic freedom is an exceptional sign of the divine image within man. For God has willed that man remain "under the control of his own decisions," so that he can seek his Creator spontaneously, and come freely to utter and blissful perfection through loyalty to Him. (*GS* 17).

10.3 Sin, Death and Our Disunity

The history of humanity shows that we have fallen from the dignity of our vocation, and our nature is wounded with disunity. Sin, according to Pope Benedict XVI, is the essential theme of the biblical understanding of the person, which, with the doctrine of the image of God, accounts for - as *Gaudium et Spes* puts it - the sense of a tragic split in our existence: 'The call to grandeur and the depths of misery are both part of human existence' (*GS* 13). God has ordained that humanity, participating in the grace of Christ through faith and the sacraments, shares in the divine nature and in the good things of God, culminating in the eternal vision of His glory. This is the source of our dignity and the measure of our tragedy when we fall into sin.

The idea of sin as disunity caused by our disruption of our vocation to communion with God, is central to the Church's experience of humanity. From this tragic account of disunity caused by sin, *Gaudium et Spes* goes on to describe our ultimate experience of disunity and lack of freedom, that is, death, as unnatural. '[Man] rightly abhors and repudiates the absolute ruin and disappearance of his own person' (*GS* 18).

This is the source of our misery - we experience the inner call to freedom and communion with God, but our history of sin presents us with the reality of disunity and dissolution and the certain knowledge that we lack the power to achieve the fundamental meaning and vocation of our lives.

10.4   Christ 'Fully Reveals Man to Man Himself' (*GS 22*)

> The truth is that only in the mystery of the incarnate Word does the mystery of man take on light. Christ, the final Adam, by the revelation of the mystery of the Father and His love, fully reveals man to man himself and makes his supreme calling clear. (*GS* 22).

The greatest truth the Church has to offer the world - drawn from her experience of divinity and humanity - is the person of Jesus Christ. Jesus is the answer in the Church's dialogue with modern man about the 'riddle of human existence' (*GS* 18) - the dignity of the human person set against the void of sin.

On the basis of this insight that 'only in the mystery of the incarnate word is light shed on the mystery of man', *Gaudium et Spes* offers us a humanism that reveals the full truth of man's dignity and vocation to communion with God.

This revelation of the mystery of the person in the incarnate word is no theory or ideology, but a fact of existence - Christ's assumption of human nature is an event which effects every human being, whether they know it or not.

> All the essential problems of man find tangible expression in the Christ of history. The Incarnation and Redemption mean that Christ entered fully into all those problems, that He took upon Himself the full weight of the burdens they impose, and that He gave them much deeper meaning, investing them with importance, nobility and purpose...Salvation was not planned and effected independently of that which is essentially human; and that which is human has the divine stamp on it – it is an image of God (cf. *Gn* 1:26). That is why for the divine work of salvation God drew on that which is human, essentially human and constitutive of man. (Karol Wojtyla, *Sign of Contradiction*, p.117).

According to Pope Benedict XVI, this restoration of the image of God in humanity by Christ gives a new significance to human action, thought, feeling, loving 'in Christ' (Joseph Ratzinger in Herbert Vorgrimler's *Commentary on the Documents of Vatican II*, p. 160). Christ's life, death and resurrection confirms in a definitive way the 'Law of Gift' at the heart of human nature. The ultimate dignity of humanity lies in our unique vocation specifically revealed in the New Testament to communion with God through self-giving love:

> This likeness reveals that man, who is the only creature on earth which God willed for itself, cannot fully find himself except through a sincere gift of himself. (*GS* 24).

10.5   The World - Reading the Signs of the Times

One of the main purposes of *Gaudium et Spes* was to present to the Church the Council Fathers judgement on the signs of the times, 'the Church has always had the duty of scrutinizing the signs of the times and of interpreting them in the light of the Gospel' (*GS* 4). Fr David Hollenbach SJ is right when he writes that the Second Vatican Council was unlike any in history in that its thousands of bishops and *periti* - theological advisers

- came from countries around the world. (David Hollenbach, in *Modern Catholic Social Teaching*). Also, it was the first to be held during the advent of the world-wide mass media, so that the world was present - so to say - in the *aula* of the Council.

Hence in *Gaudium et Spes* 4-9, the problems of the world were very much to the fore in the thinking of the Church - widespread hunger and disease, a widening and unjust gap between rich and poor nations, new forms of enslavement through social and psychological manipulation by the media, and political control by authoritarian regimes. (David Hollenbach, in *Modern Catholic Social Teaching*, p.272).

Looking at the state of the world, we can add further problems that are increasingly coming to the fore - terrorism, the trafficking of humans, global warming, environmental degradation, hunger caused by crops being diverted into bio-fuels, steep increases in the cost of commodities fuelling the potential for wars over resources.

Part Two of *Gaudium et Spes* goes on to identify five urgent problems that caused major anxiety in the 1960's. Forty years on, I believe the same five areas cause equal anxiety amongst most people:

- marriage and the family;

- culture;

- social-economic life;

- political life;

- war and peace.

Just as the Council Fathers before me, I want to encourage you all to attempt to read the signs of the times in the light of the Gospel, the Council and human experience. (*GS* 46).

10.6 MARRIAGE & FAMILY LIFE

> Personal well-being, the well-being of human and of Christian society is closely bound up with the happy condition of the marital and family community... But the dignity of this institution does not shine out equally everywhere, since it is obscured by... the plague of divorce, so-called free love and other disfigurements. Married love itself more over is profaned by egoism, hedonism and unlawful usages aimed against generation. (*GS* 47).

10.6.1 The Law of Self-Gift.

This Law of Self Gift is *the* expression of our fundamental nature because, made in the image of Trinitarian communion, we are created for interpersonal communion - 'God did not create man as a solitary' (*GS* 12).

> Loving is what we are programmed to do, what we are designed for by our Creator...This, if you like, is the programme that is hard-wired into every human person, if only we had the wisdom and generosity to live by it, if only we were

> ready to sacrifice our own preferences so as to be of service to others, to give our lives for the good of others, and above all for Jesus, who loved us and gave His life for us. (Pope Benedict XVI, World Youth Day 2008).

The Law of Self Gift is written into our physical nature as male and female. Sexuality is a profound expression of the Law of Self Gift, for God has written the meaning of total self-giving into maleness and femaleness that is predicated on marriage. Through sexual love husband and wife 'speak' the language of total self-gift that has its origin in the creative generosity and self-giving love of the Holy Trinity.

Sexuality is not purely biological, but concerns the innermost being of each person. Fidelity, permanence and openness to life are the integral conditions for total physical self-giving which is only possible for a man and a woman who have committed themselves to one another until death, as husband and wife.

Recognition of the importance of the Law of Self Gift to human existence is the reason why the Church is so adamantly against sterilisation, contraception, abortion and sex outside marriage. These acts, because they contradict and negate the God given meaning of the human person, attack the very foundations of the human world.

Sexuality is not the only dimension that manifests the significance of the Law of Self Gift. In *Gaudium et Spes* man's purpose for interpersonal communion is held up as the principal that regulates all human activity, in a way that challenges the reductionist, materialistic conception of the human person that is in the ascendancy in secular societies such as our own:

> A man is more precious for what he is than for what he has. Similarly, all that men do to obtain greater justice, wider brotherhood, a more humane disposition of social relationships has greater worth than technical advances... Hence, the norm of human activity is this: that in accord with the divine plan and will, it harmonize with the genuine good of the human race, and that it allow men as individuals and as members of society to pursue their total vocation and fulfil it. (*GS* 35).

10.6.2 The Current Situation

The following statistics provide a snap shot of the health of marriage in our country:

- There were 17.1 million families in the UK in 2006.

- Most families are headed by married couples (71%), although the proportion of cohabiting couple - families increased from 9% in 1996, to 14% in 2006.

- The average number of children per family in the UK has dropped - from 2.0 in 1971 to 1.8 in 2006.

- There were 148,141 divorces in 2006.

- Marriages in England and Wales fell by 4% to 236,980 in 2006, the lowest marriage rate since records began in 1895.

- Religious marriage ceremonies only accounted for 44% of marriages in 2006.

I believe a reliable indicator of the health of marriages is how it impacts on the well-being of children.

- More than a quarter of British under-16s regularly feel depressed. (UNICEF)

- Around 13 per cent of girls and 10 per cent of boys between 13 and 15 years old suffer from mental health problems. (UNICEF)

- More than 1,300 mentally ill children are currently being treated on adult psychiatric wards. (UNICEF).

- The NHS reports that between 2006-2007, 4,241 children under 14 attempted to commit suicide.

- 193,700 unborn children were killed through abortion in 2006; a rise of 3.9%.

- 2,000 potentially handicapped children were killed by their parents through abortion in 2006.

- A total of 40,244 abortions were carried out on girls aged between 15 and 19 years in 2006.

- 3,990 abortions were carried out on girls aged under 16 - the age of consent - in 2006.

- Teenage pregnancy rates for girls under 18 in England and Wales in 2003 was 42.3 conceptions per 1,000 girls.

These statistics reveal the shocking depth and extent of the suffering and impoverishment of so many families and children due to the separation of the unitive and procreative nature of sexual love, and the wide-spread practice of pre-marital sexual behaviour. I am convinced that there must be profoundly damaging consequences for the family in a country were contraception and abortion are so wide-spread. No wonder so many children are suffering depression and mental illness in a country that is such a hostile environment for human life. No wonder divorce is so prevalent when family life is so often characterised by a lack of generosity or self-giving love.

> For God, the Lord of life, has conferred on humans the surpassing ministry of safeguarding life in a manner which is worthy of man. Therefore from the moment of its conception life must be guarded with the greatest care while abortion and infanticide are unspeakable crimes. The sexual characteristics of man and the human faculty of reproduction wonderfully exceed the dispositions of lower forms of life... Hence when there is question of harmonizing conjugal love with the responsible transmission of life, the moral aspects of any procedure does not depend solely on sincere intentions or on an evaluation of motives, but must be determined by objective standards. (GS 51).

10.6.3 Proclaim the Theology of the Body

We, the Catholic Church, must be more confident and proactive in presenting our rich and fulfilling understanding of marriage, sexual love and the family.

The strength of the Church's doctrine of the inseparability of sexual love and procreation is that it respects the unity between the spiritual and biological dimensions of humanity. Personal meaning is informed by the biological meaning of the human body, which Pope John Paul II calls 'the language of the body'.

The Catholic theology of the body understands the meaning of married, sexual love as follows (cf. William May, *Catholic Bioethics and the Gift of Human Life*, p. 68-69):

- The Unitive Meaning: Husband and wife become personally 'one flesh' in and through sexual intercourse, renewing the covenant they made during the sacrament of marriage.

- The marital act expresses their sexual complementarity: the husband's body, which expresses his person as male, has a 'nuptial significance', for he is so structured to give himself to his wife by entering into her body, and so give himself to her. The wife's body which expresses her person as female, also has a nuptial significance, for she is so structured to receive his body into herself, and in receiving him, to give herself to him.

- ✓ The Procreative Meaning: In becoming 'one flesh' - through the sacrament of marriage - husband and wife also become one complete organism capable of generating human life. Precisely because they are married, they have capacitated themselves - according to revelation - to be co-creators with God in a way that responds to the dignity of persons - self-giving love that is faithful and permanent.

- ✓ As a people, culture and Church, we must get over misplaced shyness about sexual matters which inhibits us from spreading the Church's positive and personal vision of sexual love. We cannot leave this area of human life to the purveyors of pre-marital sex and so called safe sex to the detriment of families and young people. We have a positive message to give about the true joy of sexual love to counter the cheapening of sex by secularists. As Pope Benedict XVI puts it modesty, self-respect and moral values bring quality to human relationships. (World Youth Day 2008).

As I wrote in *Fit for Mission? Schools*, continence outside marriage and fidelity in life-long marriage are the only true and secure ways of protecting our families and young people from physical and psychological harm, such as STDs, HIV/AIDS, cervical cancer, psychological lack of self esteem and an inability to express love.

- ✓ I recommend that clergy and parents study and teach the theology of the body. I recommend the following:

  - John Paul II, *The Theology of the Body*, Boston: Pauline Books, 1997.

  - *Theology of the Body for Teens programme. www.tobforteens.com*

- Christopher West, *Theology of the Body for Beginners*, Ascension Press, 2004. *Theology of the Body Explained*, Pauline Books, 2003; *Good News about Sex and Marriage, Questions and Answers*, Charis Books, 2000.

- I also recommend the following who have developed the theology of the body: Rod Isaacs, Ruth Ashfield, Matthew Nichols, Mary Killeen, Robert Cassidy, and William Newton.

Key Four: The Church in the Modern World - Marriage & Family Life	
Areas for reflection	**Suggested Actions**
Marriage and the Family - What do I consider to be the impact on the parish of the recent trends in marriage? - How important is love in our lives? Is it more important than work or money? - Do I spend time with family and friends? - Do we pray together as a family? Do you say grace before and after meals? - Do I offer friendship to the lonely and widowed? - Do I support the Church's teaching on the inseparable link between marital love and openness to life?	- Review how the parish supports marriage and family life. - Consider reading: - John Paul II, *The Theology of the Body*, Boston: Pauline Books, 1997. - Theology of the Body for Teens programme. - Christopher West, *Theology of the Body for Beginners*, Ascension Press, 2004. *Theology of the Body Explained*, Pauline Books, 2003; *Good News about Sex and Marriage, Questions and Answers*, Charis Books, 2000. - The work of Rod Isaacs, Ruth Ashfield, Matthew Nichols, Mary Killeen, Robert Cassidy, and William Newton.

10.7 CULTURE

It is characteristic of man that he cannot achieve true and full humanity except through culture, that is by cultivating natural resources and spiritual values. Wherever human life is involved, then, nature and culture are closely connected... new ways are open of perfecting culture and spreading it widely. Enormous advances in the natural and social sciences, in the humanities, in technology, in means of communication have all contributed to this. (*GS* 54).

10.7.1 The Current Situation

The following statistics provide a snap shot of the culture in our country:

- 65% of families have a home computer.

- Almost 40 per cent of the UK male population (13 million) used pornographic websites in 2005.

- Nearly 6 in 10 children in Britain, some as young as nine, are exposed to internet pornography mostly as a result of viewing explicit websites accidentally.

- The alcohol related death rate in the UK doubled from 4,144 deaths in 1991 to 8,758 deaths in 2006.

- Of all 16- to 59-year-olds in the UK, there were four million illicit drug users and around one million Class A drug users in 2003.

- There were 2,750 deaths due to drug misuse in 2006.

- There were 18,489 gun crime offences between 2006-2007.

- There were 3,201 road accident deaths in 2005.

- In 2006, there were 5,554 suicides in adults aged 15 and over in the UK, which represented almost one per cent of the total of all deaths at ages 15 and over.

- Of the 584,791 deaths in the UK in 2004, an estimated 936 were by voluntary euthanasia.

- Since the 1990's scientific experimentation on the unborn has resulted in the deaths of 2.2 million.

10.7.2 The Culture of Death

These shocking statistics show that there is much in our modern culture that is toxic to the life of human beings. They are convincing proof that many in the United Kingdom are promoting - as Pope John Paul II so powerfully put it - a culture of death. Pornography, alcohol and drug abuse, suicide, abortion, euthanasia, gun crime and experiments on the unborn, 'poison human society, and they do more harm to those who practise them than those who suffer from the injury. Moreover, they are a supreme dishonour to the Creator' (*GS* 27).

What do we mean when we use the phrase 'culture of Death'? There is the legalised, state-sponsored culture of death, facilitated by some medical professionals, scientists, politicians and journalists. And there is the illegal, criminally facilitated culture of death that, for example, pushes drugs, trafficking in women and children for the sex industry, and facilitates degrading activities. Both the legal and illegal cultures of death reinforce and sustain each other through spreading the general darkening of conscience in society.

10.7.3 The State-sponsored Culture of Death

Pope John Paul II saw it as a new cultural climate developing around us that justifies certain crimes against life in the name of the rights of individual freedom, claiming permission and promotion by the State, so that these evil acts can be done with total freedom, even the free assistance of health-care systems:

> Choices once unanimously considered criminal and rejected by the common moral sense are gradually becoming socially acceptable. Even certain sectors of the medical profession, which by its calling is directed to the defence and care of human life, are increasingly willing to carry out these acts against the person. In this way the very nature of the medical profession is distorted and contradicted, and the dignity of those who practise it is degraded. (John Paul II, *Evangelium Vitae*, p. 8).

As Bishop of Lancaster I have recently spoken out against a crime against life that the UK Government is enacting in the most degrading way - experimentation on embryonic human beings and the creation of human-animal hybrid. As I said in my *Easter Vigil homily* (2008):

'The Prime Minister has made it clear that he wants Britain to be the world's number one centre for genetic and stem cell research. He sees it as building up the hi-tech sector of British industry and contributing to economic growth. It is good to develop British industry and foster economic growth, but not through exploiting and destroying embryonic human persons'.

'A society that seeks medical cures and economic development at the cost of human rights, human dignity and human life is 'monstrous'. It is not the defenceless, human-animal embryo, that is 'monstrous'; it is we ourselves who have become 'monsters' for allowing the exploitation of the unborn for our economic and medical gain'.

Pope Benedict XVI conveys the enormity of the degradation inflicted on humanity by the State-sponsored culture of death with these words:

> How can it be that the most wondrous and sacred human space - the womb - has become a place of unutterable violence? (Pope Benedict XVI, World Youth Day, 2008).

10.7.4 The Illegal Culture of Death

Pope John Paul II described those deceptive and false people who promote the culture of death, particularly among the young as follows:

> These are the ones who will entice you into the paths of criminality, of drug abuse, of illicit, degrading activities, of empty superficial pleasures. Firmly resist every deceitful sower of selfishness and violence. And if any one of you by chance should find yourself ensnared in the paths of evil and feel you are lost, having come back to your senses, may you find the courage to turn back to the Father's house, like the prodigal son in the Gospel: "I will arise, I will arise"'. (Pope John Paul II, *Agenda for the Third Millennium*, p. 130).

If the State is seen sponsoring crimes against life, is it any wonder that criminality in general thrives, and seeks to take advantage of the coarsening and darkening of conscience?

All of us have seen in the news the frequent reports of young people killing strangers in the street, killing fathers defending their property, killing people with learning difficulties, killing other young people who are different to them. Before going on, let me say that we're talking here about a minority of young people, and that most victims of youth crime are other young people.

"WHICH OF THESE, DO YOU THINK, WAS A NEIGHBOUR TO THE MAN WHO FELL INTO THE HANDS OF THE ROBBER?" HE SAID, "THE ONE WHO SHOWED HIM MERCY". JESUS SAID TO HIM, "GO AND DO LIKEWISE".

LUKE 10:36–37

The questions we're all asking are, 'Why are some young people so violent? Why do they have such a callous disregard for their own lives and the lives of others?'

One of the causes of the present violence lies in the promotion of a nihilistic, pleasure-seeking culture that focuses on immediate gratification. Contemporary music, films and games often portray assertive pleasure-seeking as 'normal'. Risk taking behaviour is also portrayed as glamorous and 'cool', even criminal behaviour. It seems to me that thrill-seeking is so popular because people are desperate for distractions to help them avoid the big emptiness in their lives.

Surely life means more than going from one thrill to the next, from one distraction to the next? But how do we convince others of this truth without seeming killjoys and 'boring'?

One of the ways is to show how people are being conned by consumer capitalism into missing the true, good things of life. I think we need to promote a Christian critique of modern capitalist culture. As I wrote in *Fit for Mission? A Guide*,

> We live in a culture that uses promises to excite our desire for things, keep us distracted, and leave us dissatisfied, so that we want more! We are beings orientated to Promise – our future fulfilment in the vision of God. The drama of salvation is the unfolding of God's promises to Israel and each one of us. Our very experience is transformed by God's promises. Excesses of consumer capitalism exploit our orientation to the future.
>
> Is it any wonder that we live in an increasingly angry and discontented society? It is all too common to witness people reduced to rage and indignant protest at the slightest frustration of their will or challenge to their expectations! (*Fit for Mission? A Guide*, p. 5).

I am convinced another cause of the wide-spread violence lies in the Abortion Act of 1967. For 41 years we've lived in a state-sponsored culture of death that has killed 5 million children, and we're now surprised that some of the surviving children have turned out violent with no regard for the sanctity of life?

How many children know that their mothers have had an abortion? What effect will it have on them knowing that they have been deprived of a brother or sister through abortion?

If a society holds human life so cheaply is it any surprise that young people will also hold life cheaply and engage in violence?

I encourage all our schools and parishes to continue to take steps to protect our young people from cultures of death, that seek to corrupt and exploit them.

10.7.5 Proclaim the Gospel of Life

There is one thing I know without a shadow of a doubt - the overwhelming majority of Catholics, practising or lapsed, are still strongly opposed to abortion, euthanasia and experiments on embryonic human beings.

The advocates and apologists for the culture of death dismissively accuse Catholics of being 'indoctrinated' or 'brain washed'. They are wrong. The one thing we have in common is that we value human life, because we know how much God values every human life. The value of every human life is at the heart of the Gospel, 'But God proves his love for us in that while we were still sinners Christ died for us'. (*Romans* 5:8). Every crucifix in church and home proclaims the victory of life over the culture of death. The paschal mystery of Christ, (Eucharist, passion, death and resurrection) are the ultimate expression of the Law of Self Gift:

> He asks you to give up the idols of this world and to choose Him: Him, the Love that pours total meaning into our existence and invites us to live...in the exciting experience of the gift: His gift, Christ's gift, the gift offered to each of us, and then the gift of ourselves to Him, the gift of ourselves to others, and, through others, to Him once more. Lo, the prospect of building another civilisation, a new civilisation: the civilisation of love. We are here to make a start in making this great project come true: the civilisation of love. This is Jesus' civilisation, this is the Church's civilisation, this is true Christian civilisation, this is your civilisation. (Pope John Paul II, *Agenda for the Third Millennium*, p. 129).

✓ At every opportunity proclaim the right to Life - the most fundamental human right that underpins authentic work for justice and peace (cf. Mission Priority of the *Final Proposals* of the *Fit for Mission? Parish* review).

✓ Pray, Protest and Petition the institutions that promote the culture of death - Parliament, the British Medical Association, the Royal College of Nurses, Brooke Advisory Centres, broadcasters, the tabloids and broadsheets.

✓ I also recommend that parishes support Catholic organisations, such as Life groups, that provide counselling, advice, support and hospitality to women considering abortions.

✓ Also consider actively supporting the following groups promoting the Gospel of Life: *The Society for the Protection of the Unborn Child* ; *Sisters of the Gospel of Life, Life* and other pro-life organisations.

✓ I recommend that parishes support the work of Cenacolo as a way of challenging the culture of death spread by substance-abuse.

✓ I also encourage parishes to face the reality of suffering caused by alcohol abuse, through promoting the work of their local *Alcoholics Anonymous* groups.

Key Four: The Church in the Modern World - Culture	
Areas for reflection	**Suggested Actions**
Culture • What example do I give through my drinking habits? • Do I take the risk of drinking and driving? • Is a 'seedy' club supporting the finances of the parish? • Do I use internet pornography? If so, what I am doing to break this habit? • Do I manage my anger? Do I show respect and consideration towards others? • Do I contribute to the culture of violence through my behaviour in public or at home? • Do I spend time listening to the concerns and needs of young people?	• Review the parish's co-operation with schools to challenge the culture of death among young people. • Review the parish's provision for young people. What steps is the parish taking to stop young people drifting into crime? • Review the parish's support for people with alcohol and drug addiction. • At every opportunity proclaim the Gospel of Life. Pray, Protest and Petition the institutions that promote the culture of death - Parliament, the British Medical Association, the Royal College of Nurses, Brooke Advisory Centres, broadcasters, the tabloids and broadsheets. • Support Catholic organisations, such as *Life* groups, *The Society for the Protection of the Unborn Child. www.spuc.org.uk; Sisters of the Gospel of Life. www.gospeloflifesisters* that provide counselling, advice, support, and hospitality to women considering abortions and/or promote the Gospel of Life. • Support the work of *Cenacolo* as a way of challenging the culture of death spread by substance-abuse. • Promote the work of your local *Alcoholics Anonymous* groups.

10.8 SOCIO-ECONOMIC LIFE

God intended the earth and all it contains for the use of all men and peoples, so created goods should flow fairly to all, regulated by justice and accompanied by charity... Since so many in the world suffer from hunger, the Council urges men and authorities to remember that saying of the Fathers: **'Feed a man who is dying from hunger – if you have not fed him you have killed him'**. Each as far as he can must share and spend his wealth in coming to the assistance especially of these suffering individuals or peoples so that they may thereby be enabled to go on to self-help and self-development. (*GS* 69).

10.8.1 Everybody has a Right to a Share of the Earth's Goods

The following statistics provide a snap-shot of deprivation resulting from inequality in sharing the earth's goods:

The World

- 1.2 billion people live on less than $ 1 a day.

- 2.6 billion people do not have access to a toilet.

- 9.7 million children under five died in 2006. The majority of deaths occurred in sub-Saharan Africa (4.8 million) and south Asia (3.1 million).

- 2 million children die within the first 24 hours of life.

- 6 million children could be saved if a package of low-cost health interventions were made more readily available to children and their families.

- According to James Wolfensohn, president of the World Bank, there is a 'fundamental imbalance' with the world spending US$900bn on defence; around US$325bn on agricultural subsidies and only US$60bn on aid.

UK

- 13 million people are living in low income households, which is 22% of the population.

- 3.8 million children are living in low income households.

- Around 10,000 pupils are permanently excluded from school each year. Four-fifths of permanent exclusions are boys.

- 120,000 children aged 10 to 17 were found guilty of, or cautioned for, indictable offences in 2006.

- Half of all lone parent families are on low incomes.

- 17% of pensioners live on low incomes.

Faced with these statistics, that cannot begin to convey the depth of suffering and misery of each life touched by poverty, I can't help thinking that if we were wholehearted Christians we'd know these facts as well as we know the words of the Our Father or the Hail Mary! The fact that they will be news to most of us indicates - I fear - how inward looking and self-satisfied we have become as the people of God.

Even glimpsing the enormity of suffering caused by poverty around the world and in our own country the temptation is to switch off, or give up because it appears to be a problem beyond individual action. Don't let this happen!

Another response is to feel guilt about how much we have as individuals and families, compared to how little many have in the developing countries. It is commonplace nowadays for people to reject guilt as harmful or abnormal. It isn't. Guilt is the response of the spiritual immune system to the presence of sin and evil. Let's be quite clear here, the suffering and death caused by poverty, hunger and preventable diseases is a sin that cries to heaven. More people in the rich west need to feel guilty about our unrestrained affluence, if that is the only way that action happens!

10.8.2 Will We Achieve the *Millennium Development Goals*?

Archbishop Celestino Migliore's address to the UN General Assembly concerning achieving the *Millennium Development Goals* by 2015 gives a succinct overview of the challenges facing us all. Archbishop Migliore said,

> At halfway point, while much has been done towards achieving the goals, abject poverty, hunger, illiteracy and lack of even the most basic healthcare are still rampant, indeed worsening in some regions. Tackling these challenges that continue to afflict hundreds of millions remains, therefore, at the very centre of our concerns. (*Address delivered by Archbishop Celestino Migliore, permanent observer of the Holy See to the United Nations, at the 62nd session of the U.N. General Assembly*).

Archbishop Migliore goes on to provide a summary of the challenges facing the successful implementation of the *Millennium Development Goals*:

Eradicate extreme poverty and hunger: Poverty and hunger are an offense against human dignity. However, the overall goal of reducing hunger and poverty remains elusive. While international aid is important, a fairer international trade environment - including addressing market-distorting practices that disadvantage weaker economies - is even more decisive.

Achieve universal primary education. Promote gender equality and empower women: There has been progress towards achieving universal access to primary education, with some of the poorest regions seeing a dramatic increase in enrolment. In particular, utmost efforts must be made to give equal educational opportunities to boys and girls, and to ensure that no child is left behind for purely economic and social reasons. There are 58 countries that are at risk of not receiving access to education by 2015, unless "redoubled efforts" are put forth.

The Catholic Church has long been at the forefront of providing universal access to education, with thousands of educational institutions located in run down inner city centres, remote rural communities, and 'in places where children are constrained to work to survive.'

Reduce child mortality. Improve maternal health. Combat HIV/AIDS, malaria, and other diseases. Archbishop Migliore reports that, 'While progress has been made in reducing child mortality, there has been slower progress in addressing maternal health, HIV/AIDS, malaria and tuberculosis... The overriding cause of the slow progress has been the lack of resources at the most basic levels of health care and the continued lack of access to even basic health services. It has been long demonstrated that investing in primary health care, rather than in selective, culturally divisive and ideologically driven forms of health services, which camouflage the destruction of life among medical and social services, is one of the most cost effective and successful ways to improve the overall quality of life and the stability of families and communities.'

The Catholic Church invests heavily in primary healthcare throughout the developing world, with a 'preferential option for the most under served and marginalized sectors of society.'

Many of the *UN Millennium Development Goals*, agreed by the international community, are a concrete expression of the Gospel in action. Implementation of these goals is a different matter, particularly the promotion of contraception and abortion under the euphemism, 'universal access to reproductive health'. In the light of the profoundly anti-Catholic bias and anti-Christian animosity at work in some of the institutions of the United Nations, I believe that it is vital that Catholics are vigilant as to how the aspirations of the *Millennium Development Goals* are fulfilled.

10.8.3 The Struggle for Justice and Love

Reflecting on the *Acts of the Apostles* in his encyclical, *Deus Caritas Est* (DCE), Pope Benedict XVI writes that the account of communion within the Church based on a pooling of resources (*Ac* 4:32-37) and the institution of the seven deacons (*Ac* 6:5-6), established the following three principles in the life of the Church, that:

1. The ministry of charity and social justice is equal to the proclamation of the Word and celebration of liturgy as expressions of the Church's deepest nature. (*DCE* 25).

2. 'There can never be room for a poverty that denies anyone what is needed for a dignified life'. (*DCE* 20).

3. 'As a community the Church must practise love. Love needs to be organised if it is to be an ordered service to the community'. (*DCE* 20).

Pope Benedict XVI makes it clear that the Church's action for justice and love is quite distinctive. Our work for charity and social justice is done in the name and power of

Jesus Christ. This is not the same as saying this work is done in the spirit of Gandhi or Martin Luther King, no matter how praiseworthy. When Christians work in the spirit of Jesus Christ, the Son of God, we do it 'in Christ', so that He is present and active in ways beyond our comprehension.

> Practical activity will always be insufficient, unless it visibly expresses a love for man, a love nourished by an encounter with Christ. My deep personal sharing in the needs and sufferings of others becomes a sharing of my very self with them: if my gift is not to prove a source of humiliation, I must give to others not only something that is my own, but my very self; I must be personally present in my gift. (Pope Benedict XVI, *Deus Caritas Est*, 34).

Pope Benedict proposes a number of principles that must guide our work for charity and social justice:

❖ Charity workers need a "formation of the heart": they need to be led to that encounter with God in Christ which awakens their love and opens their spirits to others.' (*DCE* 31).

❖ Christian charitable activity must be independent of parties and ideologies. It should be guided by the faith which works through love (cf. *Ga* 5:6). (*DCE* 31 & 32).

❖ Charity, furthermore, cannot be used as a means of engaging in what is nowadays considered proselytism. Love is free; it is not practised as a way of achieving other ends. (*DCE* 31).

❖ 'Prayer, as a means of drawing ever new strength from Christ, is concretely and urgently needed. People who pray are not wasting their time, even though the situation appears desperate and seems to call for action alone'. (*DCE* 36).

✓ Every parish needs to actively participate in the struggles of justice and love, through, for example, working with CAFOD and the Holy See's charity *Cor Unum*, to bring about the *UN Millennium Development Goals* in ways that are in accord with Catholic moral doctrine.

✓ The UK government is to be congratulated for its support of the International Finance Facility for Immunisation, which provides immediate funding for immunisation programmes for children under the age of 5 in the developing world. The goal is that by 2015, the lives of 10 million people in 72 countries will have been saved, 5 million of them children. Pope Benedict XVI was the first to purchase the UK bond. I encourage parishes and individuals to support the International Finance Facility programme. *http://www.iff-immunisation.org/*

✓ Following the principle that the beginning and end of our struggle for justice and love must be prayer, I call on all parishes and individuals to re-double your commitment to prayer for those that suffer poverty at home and abroad, particularly at Mass and Exposition of the Blessed Sacrament.

✓ I particularly encourage parishes and schools to work closely together on these issues, harnessing the enthusiasm of the young with the commitment of the parishes.

Key Four: The Church in the Modern World - Socio-economic Life	
Areas for reflection	**Suggested Actions**
Socio-economic Life • When buying cheap goods, such as clothing, do I consider the working conditions of the workers? • Do I regularly buy *fairtrade* goods as part of my weekly shop? • Do I purchase expensive items without giving a thought to the good that money would do given to the poor? • What percentage of my annual income do I tithe to charity? 2.5%? 1%? • What steps have I taken to reduce my carbon footprint? • If I am an employer, do I ensure that my employees receive a just wage and family friendly working conditions? • If I am an employee, do I ensure I work for my employer honestly? • What am I doing at present to contribute towards the realisation of the UN Millennium Development Gaols? • What am I doing to support the work of CAFOD, Aid to the Church in Need, and other charities? • How can I work closely with others on these issues, particularly to harness the enthusiasm of the young and the commitment of the parish?	• Review the parish's support of *fairtrade*. • Review the parish's energy consumption in order to reduce the parish's carbon foot print. • Actively contribute to CAFOD's campaigns. (At the time of writing CAFOD has launched the Unearth Justice campaign, raising awareness of the impact of the gold mining industry on communities). Also/or with the Holy See's charity *Cor Unum*, to bring about the *UN Millennium Development Goals* in ways that are in accord with Catholic moral doctrine. • Consider supporting the *International Finance Facility programme for Immunisation. http://www.iff-immunisation.org/* • Re-double your commitment to prayer for those that suffer poverty at home and abroad, particularly at Mass and Exposition of the Blessed Sacrament.

10.9 POLITICAL LIFE

> By virtue of her function and field of action the Church is quite distinct from the political community and uncommitted to any political system; she is at once the sign and the guarantee that human personality transcends the field of politics... The Church, rooted in the Redeemer's love, helps to make justice and charity flourish more vigorously within nations and between nations. She preaches the gospel of truth and brings the light of her teaching to bear on every province of human affairs with the witness of her faithful. Thus she respects and promotes political liberty and responsibility. (*GS* 76).

10.9.1 The Current Situation

The following statistics provide a snap-shot of the state of political life in our country:

- There was a 61% turnout at the 2005 General Election.

- Since 1997 the government has created over 3,023 new criminal offences.

- Since 1997 the government has passed 115,000 pages of legislation and introduced more than 50 Bills, including 24 criminal justice measures.

- In 2008 there were 82,319 inmates serving time in UK jails.

- In 2004 there were 523,580 civil servants.

- The government spent £33. 4bn on national defence between 2007-2008.

- The government spent £77 bn on education between 2007-2008.

- The government spent £90 bn on health in 2007.

- The government spent £5.3bn on overseas aid between 2007-2008.

10.9.2 Evangelising the British State

Earlier in the year I was summoned to appear before the Commons Select Committee for Children, Schools and Families to answer questions concerning my teaching document, *Fit for Mission? Schools*. Frankly, I was surprised by this intervention of the State in the life of my Diocese, but I agreed to appear before the committee of MPs for a number of reasons: first, I believe a spirit of co-operation between Church and State is vital for the well-being of our nation; second, I wanted to clear up any misunderstandings and misrepresentations that had appeared in the media; third, I will never miss an opportunity to witness to the truth of the Gospel. As *Gaudium et Spes* puts it, 'Bishops who have the task of ruling the Church of God... should preach Christ's message so as to shed the light of the Gospel on all human affairs'(*GS* 43). It is always best to assume that people will be receptive to the truth, rather than to assume they have closed minds.

Reflecting on the encounter, I was disappointed at the basic lack of knowledge exhibited by some members of the committee about Catholic education, and the Catholic

DO NOT BE CONFORMED TO THIS WORLD, BUT BE TRANSFORMED BY THE RENEWING OF YOUR MINDS, SO THAT YOU MAY DISCERN WHAT IS THE WILL OF GOD – WHAT IS GOOD AND ACCEPTABLE AND PERFECT.

ROMANS 12:2

Church in general. There appeared to be an *a priori* suspicion and scepticism about the motives and practices of faith schools in general, and Catholic schools and the Church in particular. Any hint of evangelisation or catechesis, even within our Catholic schools, is increasingly viewed as intolerable indoctrination and proselytism.

I came away concerned that a breach seems to be growing between the State and the Church, and the position of faith in general, which will harm the ability of both to help the citizens of our county to 'fulfil their personal and social vocation.' As *Gaudium et Spes* puts it, 'the more they co-operate reasonably...the more effectively they will perform this service to everybody's advantage.' (*GS* 76).

We must work harder to convince the State of the invaluable role of religion in society. As Pope Benedict XVI puts it,

> ...to become more aware of the irreplaceable role of religion for the formation of consciences and the contribution which it can bring to - among other things - the creation of a basic ethical consensus in society. (Pope Benedict XVI, *Address at the Elysée Palace*, France, September 2008)

Of one thing I am certain, this breach will not be mended though compromising the faith and morals of Catholic doctrine. What is needed is evangelisation of state power through 'its confrontation with the abiding objectivity of the natural moral law, itself an expression of the divine Wisdom, and the measure of all positive law on earth.' (Aidan Nichols, *The Realm*, p.147). Pope Benedict XVI sets us an example of how to use natural law in our dialogue with politicians and the State:

> The Universal Declaration of Human Rights are based on the natural law inscribed on human hearts and present in different cultures and civilizations. Removing human rights from this context would mean restricting their range and yielding to a relativistic conception, according to which the meaning and interpretation of rights could vary and their universality would be denied in the name of different cultural, political, social and even religious outlooks. This great variety of viewpoints must not be allowed to obscure the fact that not only rights are universal, but so too is the human person, the subject of those rights. (Address of His Holiness Benedict XVI, *Meeting with the Members of the General Assembly of the United Nations Organisation*, 18th April 2008).

10.9.3 Anti-Catholicism - The Last Acceptable Prejudice

It is widely recognised that one of the achievements of Cardinal Basil Hume was to place the Catholic Church in the mainstream of British political and institutional life. There have been obvious benefits to the Church, such as giving Catholics a voice in national decision-making.

However, I suspect that we have all been slightly dazzled by the glamour of power, and have forgotten that we still have enemies in a country that has a long history of anti-Catholicism. What Archbishop Charles Chaput writes about America equally applies here, maybe even more so: '...Catholics have ignored an unpleasant truth: that there are active, motivated groups...that bitterly resent the Catholic Church and the Christian Gospel, and would like to silence both'. (Charles Caput, *Render unto Caesar*, p.187).

I am sure some will say I'm scaremongering or paranoid, and thereby try to discredit or marginalise what I write. However, over the years I have read some quite foul things written about the Catholic Church and nasty personal attacks against Pope John Paul II and Pope Benedict XVI in respectable national broadsheet newspapers and on TV, which would just not have appeared in print or on the TV if they were about other religions or religious figures.

Another example of the hostility of the media towards the Catholic Church is their relentless promotion of the falsification of history when they assert that Pope Pius XII did nothing to assist the Jewish people during the Holocaust and even collaborated with the Nazis'. Though it may be true that as Nuncio to Germany before the war, he - like many others - underestimated the threat posed by Hitler and the Nazis regime, this does not mean he was a sympathetic fellow traveller.

The crude fabrication that Pope Pius XII was anti-Semitic, and was passive before the Holocaust, has become an unquestioned 'fact'. So much so that when the world-renowned Jewish historian Sir Martin Gilbert, and expert on the Holocaust, published his exhaustive work, *The Righteous*, proving 'the true and wonderful achievements of Catholics in helping Jews during the war', under the active leadership of Pope Pius XII, it went largely ignored by the world's media.

One cannot help but wonder at the motives of those who perpetrate this gross misrepresentation of the Church's history. For instances, why do they ignore the historic fact that the former Prime Minister of Israel, Golda Meir, made this statement about Pope Pius XII, which counters the slander that he was the 'Silent Pope'?

> 'When fearful martyrdom came to our people in the decade of Nazi terror, the voice of the Pope was raised for the victims. The life of our times was enriched by a voice speaking out on the great moral truths above the tumult of daily conflict. We mourn a great servant of peace.' (Sir Martin Gilbert, *Hitler's Pope?* in *The American Spectator*. (July/August 2006).

Furthermore, I couldn't help but notice that when I was called before the House of Commons Select Committee to defend Faith schools only Christians were required to respond to the ill-informed accusation of unfair selection, even though there are Jewish and Muslim Faith schools. Under the slogan of 'multi-culturalism', institutions - such as national and local government, education, and the media - show a tendency to criticise and marginalise Christianity, while at the same time respecting and celebrating other world faiths.

Professor Philip Jenkins, an American Episcopalian, has written a powerful book called, *The New Anti-Catholicism: The Last Acceptable Prejudice*. In this work he shows how American politics, education and media have promoted sensitivity about the treatment and portrayal of ethnic, religious and sexual groups, which are not applied equally to the Catholic faith. I am convinced that what Professor Jenkins identifies in American culture, equally applies in Great Britain:

> Over the years, we have come to expect that media treatments of the Church, its clergy and its faithful will be negative, if not highly offensive, and Catholic organizations try to confront the worst manifestations of prejudice. When such controversies erupt, the defenders of the various shows or productions commonly invoke a free speech defence. These productions are just legitimate commentary, we hear, so offended Catholics should just lighten up, and learn not to be hyper-sensitive. Sometimes, defenders just deny that the allegedly anti-Catholic works are anything like as hostile as they initially seem to be. All these arguments, though, miss one central point, namely that similarly controversial attacks would be tolerated against literally no other group, whether that group is religious, political or ethnic. (Philip Jenkins, '*Some Prejudices are more equal than others*' in *Catalyst*, 2003).

Anti-Catholicism is one expression of a more general Christianophobia which is spreading throughout the world. I agree whole heartedly with Archbishop Dominique Mamberti, Secretary of the Secretariat of State, when he states that 'discrimination against Christians is as equally unacceptable as anti-Semitism and Islamophobia, and should be resisted with the same force.' Christianophobia refers to acts of violence, persecution, intolerance and discrimination against Christians.

Archbishop Mamberti observes that, 'In many countries Christians are victims of prejudice, stereotypes and intolerance, at times of a cultural nature. It's a paradox not to guarantee Christians the same freedoms granted to other religions, or to create a sort of hierarchy of intolerances'.

What should be our response to this re-emergence of anti-Catholicism as an acceptable prejudice? Archbishop Charles Chaput offers penetrating analysis and recommendations:

➢ We should not soften the Christian message - the cross, the call to holiness, the need for salvation from sin - just because 'these truths aren't considered respectful in a secular, pluralistic society'.

➤ The danger is that to gain a public hearing, Catholics justify the church's social teaching in practical, humanitarian terms, not explicitly founded on the Gospel of Jesus Christ.

➤ Catholics must not allow the hostility of the secular world make us abridge the Gospel, cutting out the proclamation of Jesus Christ, the unique saviour of the world.

> What needs to be done by Catholics today for their country? The answer is: *Don't lie.* If we say we're Catholic, we need to prove it ... public life needs people willing to stand alone, without apologies, for the truth of the Catholic faith and the common human values it defends. One person can make a difference - if that individual has a faith her or she is willing to suffer for; a faith that can say, as [St John] Fisher did in greeting his executioner "I come to die for the faith of Christ and Christ's Catholic Church." (Charles Chaput, *Render unto Caesar*, p. 197).

10.9.4 Loving our Neighbour has Political Implications

The Church is not a political organization. She has no interest in partisanship because getting power or running governments is not what she's about, and the more closely she identifies herself with any single party, the fewer people she can effectively reach.

However, Scripture and Tradition *do* have public consequences because they guide us in how we should act. The Catholic faith has social justice implications - and that means it also has cultural, economic and political implications. Loving God requires that we also love the people He created, which means we need to treat them with justice, charity and mercy. Being a Catholic involves solidarity with other people.

We can't call ourselves Catholic and then simply stand by while migrants get mistreated, or the poor get robbed, or unborn children get killed. The Catholic faith is always personal, but never private.

If our faith is real, then it will bear fruit in our public decisions and behaviours, including our political choices. But how do we make good political choices when so many different issues are so important and complex? The first principle of Christian social thought is: *Don't deliberately kill the innocent, and don't collude in allowing somebody else to do it.* The right to life is the foundation of every other human right. This is why the issues of abortion, euthanasia, international aid and war are so important for Catholics when it comes to deciding how to vote.

So can a Catholic in good conscience vote and campaign for a political candidate who supports and promotes abortion and/ or euthanasia or promotes a cut in international aid? My personal answer to this question is: *I can't and I won't.* But I do know some serious Catholics - people whom I admire on a whole range of issues - who will vote and campaign for MPs who hold all kinds of positions that are against the teachings of the Church. I know that they do sincerely struggle with their party's position on, say, abortion or stem-cell research, and it causes them real pain. More importantly: *They don't keep quiet about it!* They re-double their efforts to bring about reform of their party's position.

In my opinion, it is only in these very strict circumstances that it is permissible to support and vote for a Member of Parliament who holds positions against the teaching of the Church. It is never permissible to casually vote for a candidate without knowing their stance on these issues, or to vote for them and leave it at that.

- I earnestly call on all Catholics to support politicians who are opposed to abortion, euthanasia, research on embryonic human beings, or promote an increase in international aid, the support of migrants or campaign for the *UN Millennium Goals*.

- If all the candidates are anti-life then consider voting for the candidate who is most in sympathy with Catholic social teaching, for example on the question of international aid. However, never tire of campaigning to change the candidates mind on these life issues.

- Above all follow your conscience, informed by the teaching of the Church. It may be that you cannot vote for any candidate.

Key Four: The Church in the Modern World - Political Life	
Areas for reflection	**Suggested Actions**
Political Life • What am I and my parish doing to support the growing number of ex-prisoners in our communities? • Do I visit my local prison? • Do I contribute to campaigns for prison reform? How do we move away from the mentality that sees locking more and more people up in prison as the answer to society's problems? • Do I know how my parish cares for the sick and housebound in my community? Do I know how we care for the spiritual needs of the sick in hospital and care homes? • Does my Parish have a good relationship with its local primary and secondary schools? How do I help that relationship?	• If there is a prison nearby, review the parish's pastoral care of prisoners. • Review the parish's pastoral care of sick in hospital and at home. • Consider your support for politicians who are opposed to abortion, euthanasia, research on embryonic human beings, or promote an increase in international aid, the support of migrants or campaign for the *UN Millennium Goals*. • If *all* the candidates are anti-life then consider voting for the candidate who is most in sympathy with Catholic social teaching. Never tire of campaigning to change the candidates mind on these life issues.

10.10 WAR & PEACE

> We should not be deceived by false hopes. Unless enmities and hatreds are put aside and firm and sincere agreements for universal peace are concluded, humanity, already in grave danger in spite of its marvellous scientific attainments, may reach that fatal hour in which it will not know peace but that of a terrible death. Nonetheless, the Church of Christ places herself at the heart of contemporary anxieties, and while she issues these warnings she does not cease to hope resolutely. She is determined to put to our age repeatedly, in season and out of season, the apostolic message: 'Behold now is the acceptable time' for a change of heart; 'behold now is the day of salvation. (*GS* 82).

10.10.1   The Current Situation

- An estimated 72 million people were killed during the Second World War.

- An estimated 23 million people have been killed in wars since the end of the Second World War, with tens of millions made homeless, and countless millions injured and bereaved.

- During 1990s an estimated 2 million children were killed, 4 to 5 million children disabled, 12 million children left homeless, and more than 1 million orphaned.

- International wars and civil wars in the 1990s forced 50 million people to flee their homes.

- More than 500 million small arms and light weapons are in circulation around the world - one for about every 12 people.

- It is estimated that there are between 60 and 70 million landmines in the ground in at least 70 countries.

- Despite the end of the cold war, there remain approximately 30,000 nuclear warheads, 5,000 of which are on hair-trigger alert.

- War has killed over 655,000 Iraqis or more than 500 people a day since the coalition invasion of Iraq.

10.10.2   The Brave Work of Making Peace the Highest Work of Love

It is only 63 years since the end of the last total war that raged across the world. A war that saw the destruction of whole cities, the killing of 45 million civilians, and the genocide of the Jewish people. It was a crime against God and man. As Pope John Paul II called it, 'an abyss of violence, destruction and death unlike anything previously known'. (Pope John Paul II, *Message World Day of Peace*, 2004).

The guns of the Second World War fell silent in Europe 63 years ago, the bombers stopped bombing, the soldiers and civilians stopped dying, but I am convinced 63 years later we are a society that remains traumatised and brutalised by the grief and horror of that war. We have been left a violent people that - consciously or unconsciously - see violence as a solution to problems.

Fr Thomas Cullinan provides an insightful analysis of our predilection for violence (cf. Thomas Cullinan, *The Passion of Political Love*, p.25-26). He says violence in our society has three temperatures - hot violence, cool violence and cold violence.

Hot Violence. The 250 wars since the end of World War II have been outbreaks of hot violence. At present our country is an active participant in hot violence in Afghanistan and Iraq. All the time our country is planning and practising for engagement in hot violence, with £33.4bn invested in national defence between 2007 and 2008. Towns around our diocese - Barrow and Warton - are directly involved in preparations for hot violence, manufacturing submarines, jet fighters and howitzers.

Cold Violence. Cullinan defines 'cold violence' as the deliberate use of economic power to dominate or to destroy those who lack it. He gives the example of those multi-national companies who use the 'cold violence' of their economic power to drive people from their land, such as an international tyre company establishing beef ranches in Brazil through the dislocation of people who had lived on the land for centuries.

Cool Violence. This is the subtle and unquestioned aggression that pervades our society, which is driven by an overriding concern for economic prosperity, security and the exercise of individual freedom.

It is 'cool' because its language is plausible, polite and temperate; 'market forces', 'my rights as an individual', 'my quality of life', 'trickle-down effect', 'collateral damage', 'uterine contents', 'foetal material', 'stem cell research'. Our society uses language to hide the reality and consequences of cool violence to make it appear normal and unexceptional so that it can occur unremarked and unimpeded.

The death of 10 million children every year due to preventable diseases or the 'silent holocaust' of 5 million unborn children in the UK since 1967 are the ultimate expressions of the cool violence that pervades the fabric of our society; a violence that is masked by polite, 'commonsense', no-nonsense language, while most of us - even Catholics who should know better - go about our lives untroubled and unconcerned by the vast, hidden suffering that surrounds us.

Our unquestioning acquiescence to cool violence, also enables cold violence to be a business practice, and sows the seeds for hot violence around the world.

10.10.3 Create a True Culture of Peace

Peace is not the mere absence of war... There can be no peace on earth unless personal welfare is safeguarded and men spontaneously and confidently exchange the riches of their minds and genius. The construction of peace absolutely demands a firm resolve to respect other men and peoples, and the practical determination to be brothers. Thus peace is also the fruit of love, which advances beyond what justice can supply. Earthly peace, which comes from love of our fellow-men, is a type and result of the peace of Christ issuing from God the Father. (*GS* 78).

In order to begin to create a culture of peace, we first have to recognise and speak the truth about the society in which we live - if we are honest we must admit that we are not at peace with other countries, we are not at peace with each other, or even at peace with ourselves.

Pope John Paul II was one of the great advocates and exemplars of making peace in the 20th century. Over and over again he proclaimed that true peace is founded on truth and love. The two cannot be separated, without destroying the meaning or effectiveness of both. Here is a simple action plan to make a start at finding peace in a violent society, given us by Jesus, the Prince of Peace:

❖ Speak the truth with love (*Ep* 4:15). Challenge the language of cool violence that saturates the media, public life and our personal lives.

❖ Love one another as I have loved you. Daily meditate on the life of Jesus in scripture and tradition, so as to imitate His way of being human.

❖ Love your enemies. Return violence with love.

❖ Pray daily for the gifts of the Holy Spirit, 'the fruit of the Spirit is love, joy, peace'. (*Ga* 5:22).

❖ 'Christ's peace can only be established where people are disposed to forsake sin. The deepest cause of every disagreement in the world is people's abandoning God. They who do not live at peace with God can only with difficulty live at peace with their neighbour'. (Pope John Paul II, *Agenda for the Third Millennium*, p. 196).

✓ The reality on the ground is that the defence industry, such as BAE Systems, is vital to our economic well being, providing employment for many members of our community. Sometimes they are the only major employer in a town. At the same time, we mustn't turn a blind eye to the other reality that weapons from the UK have brought death, destruction and injury to people around the world. I feel that we are called to make reparation for our co-operation in war. I invite you to contact me with suggestions about how we make reparation as a people to the Lord as a people chosen as His own and to those harmed by weapons made in our communities.

Key Four: The Pastoral Constitution on the Church in the Modern World	
Areas for reflection	**Suggested Actions**
War and Peace • How the Church make reparation as a people for our cooperation in war? • Do I contribute to campaigns that tackle the injustices that cause war? • Do I support Pax Christi?	• Review the parish's support of charities that support peace, such as Pax Christi. • Challenge the language of 'cool violence'. • Daily meditate on the life of Jesus in scripture and tradition, so as to imitate His way of being human. • Pray daily for the gifts of the Holy Spirit, 'the fruit of the Spirit is love, joy, peace'. (*Ga* 5:22).

11 Conclusion

> Go and learn what this means, 'I desire mercy, not sacrifice.' For I have come to call not the righteous but sinners. (*Mt* 9:13).

There are some things in life which are so important that to dissent from them is to lose the whole meaning of life. I have written this document in the hope that we may realise with joy the great gift with which we have been entrusted.

When we all hold true to the beauty and truth of the Church established by Jesus, for the glory of the Father, in the living presence of the Holy Spirit, then the true glory of God's Church will shine out for all to see. Our Church will be as intended, a creative and liberating force that takes us out into the world and which releases the world from the 'pains of creation' to realise its full potential.

> For the creation waits with eager longing for the revealing of the children of God; for the creation was subjected to futility, not of its own will but by the will of the one who subjected it, in hope that the creation itself will be set free from its bondage to decay and will obtain the freedom of the glory of the children of God. (*Rm* 8:19-21).

12 Appendix A: Glossary

	Definition
Aggiornamento	Bringing up to date, expressed through a critical and compassionate openness to the modern world
Charism	Graces of the Holy Spirit which directly or indirectly benefit the Church, ordered as they are to her building up, to the good of men, and to the needs of the world. (*CCC* 799).
Doctrine	Church teaching in all its many forms which is intended not only to communicate orthodox beliefs but to feed Christian life and worship. (O'Collins & Farrugia *A concise dictionary of Theology*).
Dogma	The Church's Magisterium exercises the authority it holds from Christ to the fullest extent when it defines dogmas, that is, when it proposes, in a form obliging the Christian people to an irrevocable adherence of faith, truths contained in divine Revelation or also when it proposes, in a definitive way, truths having a necessary connection with these. There is an organic connection between our spiritual life and the dogmas. Dogmas are lights along the path of faith; they illuminate it and make it secure. (*CCC* 88-89).
Encyclical	A teaching letter from the Pope.
Ecclesiology	Study of the Church.
Ecclesiology of communion	An ecclesiology which defines the Church as an organic whole composed of spiritual bonds (faith, hope and charity), and of visible structural forms (the profession of faith, the sacramental economy, the pastoral ministry), and which culminates in the Eucharistic mystery, the source and expression of the unity of the Church, or rather of the one Church. Each of these elements is considered in so far as it promotes, conditions, realises or brings about 'communion' which is the Church.

	Definition
Hermeneutic	Interpretation, the theory and practise of understanding and interpreting texts.
Magisterium	The teaching office of the Church.
Post-conciliar	After the Second Vatican Council.
Ressourcement	Return to the sources of Catholic theology and life
'Sense of the Faithful' *Sensus Fidelium*	The entire body of the faithful, anointed as they are by the Holy One, cannot err in matters of belief. They manifest this special property by means of the whole people's supernatural discernment in matters of faith when "from the Bishops down to the last of the lay faithful" they show universal agreement in matters of faith and morals. That discernment in matters of faith is aroused and sustained by the Spirit of truth. It is exercised under the guidance of the sacred teaching authority, in faithful and respectful obedience to which the people of God accepts that which is not just the word of men but truly the word of God. Through it, the people of God adheres unwaveringly to the faith given once and for all to the saints, penetrates it more deeply with right thinking, and applies it more fully in its life. (*LG* 12).
Virtue of hope	Hope is the theological virtue by which we desire the kingdom of heaven and eternal life as our happiness, placing our trust in Christ's promises and relying not on our own strength, but on the help of the grace of the Holy Spirit... The virtue of hope responds to the aspiration to happiness which God has placed in the heart of every man; it takes up the hopes that inspire men's activities and purifies them so as to order them to the Kingdom of heaven; it keeps man from discouragement; it sustains him during times of abandonment; it opens up his heart in expectation of eternal beatitude. Buoyed up by hope, he is preserved from selfishness and led to the happiness that flows from charity. (*CCC* 1817-8).

13   Appendix B: List of Church Documents

Conciliar Church documents are known by their opening words. Since they are universally available in Latin, by custom they are normally known by the opening words in Latin.

Ref	Name		Opening English Words
DV	*Dei Verbum*	*The Dogmatic Constitution on Divine Revelation*	Hearing the Word of God
GS	*Gaudium et Spes*	*The Pastoral Constitution On the Church in the Modern World*	The joys and the hopes
LG	*Lumen Gentium*	*The Dogmatic Constitution on the Church*	Christ is the light of humanity
SC	*Sacrosanctum Concilium*	*The Constitution on the Sacred Liturgy*	The sacred Council

Note: CCC = *Catechism of the Catholic Church*

14   Appendix C: Summary of Action Points in each section

Please note: Action Points are addressed to all members of the Church and, although, some of these actions may fall more naturally to the ordained ministry, do take time to ensure you prioritise those actions which most closely fall to the role the Holy Spirit is asking you to undertake. Do not immediately or lightly dismiss actions without seeking in prayer to discern the will of God.

A Study Course on *Fit for Mission? Church* for Discussion Groups.

The following 11 sessions have been designed to help you look at some key themes of *Fit for Mission? Church*. As well as selecting extracts to be examined by the group, it suggests a range of questions. Please don't feel obliged to answer all the questions. Each session can be covered in one meeting or split over a number of meetings. Many important themes and sections are not examined, so please feel free to develop your own courses of study.

SESSION ONE. HOPE AND THE HOLY SPIRIT.

Aim: Examine the importance of hope and confidence in the assistance of the Holy Spirit in our lives as Catholics. **Look at the following extracts:**

1.1 God's gift of hope. *Questions:* Am I a person of hope? Have I cultivated the virtue of hope that I received at baptism? Do I pray for the virtue of hope? Have I hope enough to face the reality of our church fairly and squarely?

2.2 The Holy Spirit inspired Vatican II. *Questions:* Where do I see signs of the Holy Spirit at work in my life? What is the Holy Spirit asking me to do? Consider the lay organisations available in my local area and whether the Holy Spirit is calling me to membership of one of these.

3.4 A Growth in understanding. *Questions:* Do I seek, through contemplation and study, to understand the spiritual reality of my life? How do I avoid the temptation of setting up my own interpretation of the faith in opposition to the sure gift of truth in the Church? How do I ensure I am open to the life giving presence of the Holy Spirit?

SESSION TWO. REASONS TO BE CHEERFUL.

Aim: Examine signs of growth and development in the Church as a result of the Second Vatican Council. **Look at the following extracts:**

2.4 A Time of Confidence and Communion. *Questions:* What do I see as signs of confidence and communion in the Church? How has the Second Vatican changed my life for the good?

7.1 Balancing Change and Continuity in the Liturgy. *Questions:* How do I participate in the liturgy? How do I prepare to participate in the liturgy?

8.2 Keeping the Bible Alive. *Questions:* What role does Scripture play in my life? Do I study the Bible? Do I pray with the Bible? What would help me get more out of the Bible?

SESSION THREE. WHERE THINGS HAVE GONE WRONG.

Aim: Examine signs of discord and confusion in the life of the Church. **Look at the following extracts:**

2.5 A Time of Discord and Confusion. *Questions:* What do I see as the signs of confusion and discord in the Church today? How has the discord and dissent in the Church affected my life as a Catholic?

4 Have we forgotten what it is to be Catholic? - 4.1 Wake from the Forgetfulness of Sleep. *Questions:* How do I ensure that I do not forget that I am a Catholic? How do I actively live my life so I am mindful of the joy and responsibility I have as a Catholic?

4.7 Rich Christians in a Hungry World - 4.8 Fully Embracing Life. *Questions:* What is my attitude to wealth and poverty? What role does the Church's teaching on social issues play in my life? What is my attitude to the Church's teaching on contraception? What role does the Church's teaching on sexuality play in my life?

SESSION 4. WHAT DID THE SECOND VATICAN COUNCIL REALLY SAY?

Aim: Examine the purpose of the Second Vatican Council so as to better distinguish between authentic and inauthentic interpretations. **Look at the following extracts:**

3.1.1 Henri Cardinal de Lubac SJ. *Questions:* What is Tradition in the Church? How important is the tradition of the Church to your life as a Catholic? What would you say are the essential traditions of the Church? How do we balance change with continuity of tradition?

3.1.3 Pope John Paul II. *Questions:* Why is the new *Catechism* important to the future of the Church? What role does the new *Catechism* play in my life? Do I study the new *Catechism*? What would help me get more out of the *Catechism*?

3.1.4 Pope Benedict XVI. *Questions:* Do you think the Second Vatican Council created a new Catholic Church? Why would it matter if we broke with the past? Has your parish managed to embrace the new, while being true to the past?

SESSIONS 5 & 6. WHAT DOES IT MEAN TO BE A CATHOLIC?

Aim: To know the essential elements of being a Roman Catholic. **Look at the following extracts:**

4.3.1 Inner Communion of Faith, Hope and Love. *Questions:* Would others say I strive for a life of faith, hope and love? Do I love the Church? Do I have a lightness of being, a generosity of Spirit, a readiness for genuine laughter, a willingness to go the extra mile for anyone, or any cause? Do I remain in the presence of love?

4.3.2 External Communion of Creed, Liturgy and Discipline. *Questions:* What is the meaning of 'Catholic'? What is the opposite of being Catholic?

4.4 Professing the Faith. *Questions:* Do I prefer my own subjective, personal understanding of the faith over the teachings of the Church? What would help me come to a greater understanding and appreciation of the Church's teaching? How do I keep up-to-date with the Pope's latest teaching? Am I really a believing Catholic?

4.5 Celebrating the Sacraments. *Questions:* Do I regularly participate in the Sunday celebration of the Mass? When was the last time I studied the meaning of the different parts of the Mass? Do I regularly participate in the sacrament of reconciliation? Or do I think God will forgive my sins if I just ask for His forgiveness? Why is it necessary for priests and deacons to receive the sacrament of Holy Orders?

4.6 Recognising the Authority of the Pope and Bishops. *Questions:* Do I respect the authority of the Pope and bishop to teach me about the truths of faith and morality? Do I recognise my duty to contribute my opinion, based on knowledge or gifts, concerning the good of the Church? What is meant by the term 'sense of the faithful' [*sensus fidelium*]?

4.9 The Dialogue of Obedience. *Questions:* What do I think when I hear the word 'obedience'? What role did obedience play in the life of Jesus? In what ways are the Pope, bishops, priests and deacons meant to be obedient? Do I participate in Christ's spirit of obedience to the truth given Him by the Father? What would help me develop an attitude of obedience to the truth of Catholic doctrine and morals?

SESSION 7. THE CHURCH IS NOT MAN-MADE, IT COMES FROM GOD.

Aim: Deepen our appreciation of the origin of the Church in the Holy Trinity. **Look at the following extracts:**

5. The Church is the Work of the Holy Trinity. *Questions:* Have I got into the habit of just thinking of the Church as a human institution? What difference does it make to be aware of the origin and life of the Church in the Holy Trinity?

5.1 God is One. *Questions:* Why is unity important to the nature of God? Why is the unity of the Church important? What do I need to do to remain united to the Catholic Church? What can I do to preserve the unity of the Church?

5.3 God the Father. *Questions:* What is the Father's plan for the human race? What do creation and salvation tell us about the Father's attitude to the human race? What is the Church's role in the Father's plan for the human race? What is the Father's plan for my life?

5.4 God the Son. *Questions:* What is the Son's role in the Father's plan for the human race? How is the Church the sacramental sign of the Incarnation? What is the Kingdom of God? How does Christ's sacrifice on the Cross and the Mass make the Kingdom of God present?

5.5 God the Holy Spirit. *Questions:* Where do I meet the Holy Spirit? How is the Holy Spirit at work in the Church? Do I give any thought to what I received through the sacrament of confirmation? What gifts for the Church have I received from the Holy Spirit?

SESSION 8. HOW DO WE GET LITURGY RIGHT?

Aim: Examine ways liturgy can go wrong, and ways to get it right. **Look at the following extracts:**

7.2.1 The Shadow of False Freedom - 7.2.2 The Light of Obedience. *Questions:* What is the primary purpose of liturgy - worship of God or human interest? Why is it important to have rules about hope to celebrate the Mass? Why does the Church say it is a misuse of liturgy to add innovations? Why do some people have difficulty in following the rules about the liturgy?

7.2.3 The Shadow of Ignorance - 7.2.4 The Light of Doctrine. *Questions:* How do I view Jesus - God made man or a special man? Do I keep my 'focus' on God during the Mass? Do I attain self-forgetfulness in worship? What helps and hinders me in this? How can I deepen my knowledge and awareness of God in the liturgy?

7.2.5 The Shadow of Consumerism - 7.2.6 The Light of True Faith. *Questions:* Does the celebrant of the liturgy have to entertain in order to keep the interest of the community? Do I need novelty and stimulation to stay interested in the liturgy? Do I shop around to find liturgy that suits my personal taste? What does it mean to describe the Mass as a Holy Sacrifice? What do I understand when Christ's sacrifice is described as "that full restoration of what has been taken from God through man's sin, His honour and glory"?

SESSION 9. STAYING FAITHFUL TO THE WORD OF GOD.

Aim: To know the Catholic approach to Scripture so as to avoid the pitfalls of dissent and the misuse of scripture. **Look at the following extracts:**

8.3 The Risk of Misusing the Bible - 8.4 The True use of Scripture. *Questions:* Do I think that all I need is the Bible to understand God's revelation? If I don't understand something in the Bible where do I go to find out more? The new *Catechism*? Why is it important to read Scripture in the light of Catholic Tradition? How do I find out about and follow Church Tradition? Am I aware of the difference between Tradition and traditions ? What is essential to the identity of the Church and what is time-conditioned and changeable?

8.5 The Risk of Growing Dissent - 8.6 Right to the Purity and Integrity of the Faith. *Questions:* Am I sceptical about the supernatural dimension of Scripture? Do I believe God acts in the world? Do I believe the God became man? Do I believe in miracles? Do I believe that the Gospels contain eye-witness testimony about Jesus? Or do I believe that claims about Jesus' divinity where added by later generations of Christians? Do I doubt that the Catholic Church preserves the fullness of truth about God and humanity? Do I indulge in speculations unsupported by proper reference to the teaching of the Catholic Church? How do I develop strategies and counter-measures to protect myself from forces that are destructive of faith?

SESSION 10. ONE, HOLY, CATHOLIC, AND APOSTOLIC CHURCH.

Aim: To have a Catholic understanding of the Church. **Look at the following extracts:**

9.3 Threats to the Communion of the Church - The Church of Christ subsists in the Catholic Church. *Questions:* Do I have a Catholic understanding of the Church? Do I believe that Jesus instituted the Catholic Church? Can we change the Church as we see fit? Do I consider the Catholic Church unique, or just one church among many churches?

9.4 Threats to Genuine Ecumenism - 9.5 The Genuine Understanding of Communion - 9.7 Elements of the Church outside the Catholic Church. *Questions:* Do I look on non Catholic churches and communities as variously participating in the communion of the one Church of Christ? Do I value the distinct spiritualities and traditions of other non Catholic churches?

SESSION 11. PEOPLE OF LIFE IN A CULTURE OF DEATH.

Aim: To know the extent of the Culture of Death that dominates our society, so as to better witness to the Gospel of Life. **Look at the following extracts:**

10.7.1 The Current Situation. *Questions:* How has the Culture of Death touched my life? How I feel living in a society that is so destructive of human life and happiness? What gives me hope?

10.7.2 The Culture of Death - 10.7.3 The State-sponsored Culture of Death - 10.7.4 The Illegal Culture of Death. *Questions:* Does the State promote a moral society? To what extent is the Government responsible for the Culture of Death? What is the role of the Church in a society dominated by the Culture of Death? What is my responsibility?

10.7.5 Proclaim the Gospel of Life/10.9.2 Evangelise the British State-10.9.3 Loving our Neighbours has Political Implications. *Questions:* Does abortion, euthanasia, oversees aid determine how I vote in an election? Would I vote for a politician who opposed Church morality? Do I lack courage to proclaim the Catholic teaching on life? Do I let my fear of hostility, ridicule, or scornful indifference get the better of me? Am I afraid of being unpopular or shunned for appearing in the eyes of some of being fundamentalist, ignorant or religious?